EXPLORING
THE RIDGEWAY

G000109218

EXPLORING
THE RIDGEWAY

Alan Charles

COUNTRYSIDE BOOKS
NEWBURY, BERKSHIRE

First published 1988
© Alan Charles 1988
Reprinted 1989

All rights reserved.
No reproduction permitted
without the prior permission
of the publishers:

COUNTRYSIDE BOOKS
3 Catherine Road
Newbury, Berkshire
ISBN 1 85306 009 7

Cover Photograph of Roden Down taken by the author
Sketch Maps by the author
Line drawings by Leonard J Hayes R.I.B.A.

Produced through MRM (Print Consultants) Ltd., Reading
Typeset by SOS Typesetting, Reading
Printed in England by JW Arrowsmith Ltd., Bristol

Contents

THE RIDGEWAY PATH

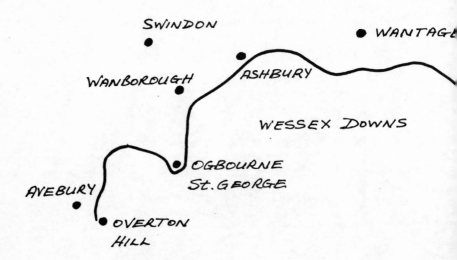

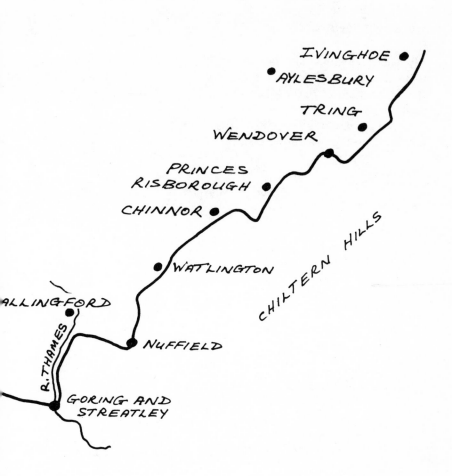

IVINGHOE

AYLESBURY

TRING

WENDOVER

PRINCES
RISBOROUGH

CHINNOR

WATLINGTON

CHILTERN HILLS

ALLINGFORD

R. THAMES

NUFFIELD

GORING AND
STREATLEY

Acknowledgements

My sincere thanks to David Venner, the Ridgeway Officer at Oxfordshire County Council, for his unstinted help and advice during the preparation of this book, and to all those who helped me in so many ways.

I am very grateful to my wife, Betty, for her valiant service (and patience!) at the word-processsor.

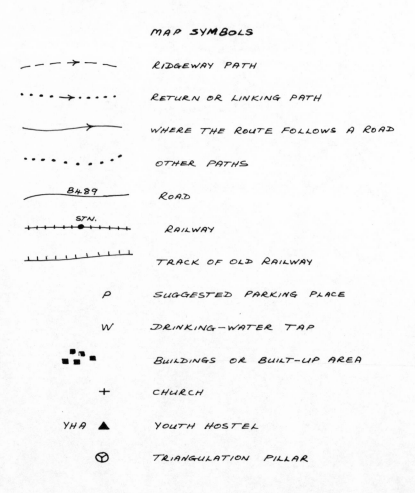

MAP SYMBOLS

RIDGEWAY PATH

RETURN OR LINKING PATH

WHERE THE ROUTE FOLLOWS A ROAD

OTHER PATHS

B489 ROAD

STN. RAILWAY

TRACK OF OLD RAILWAY

P SUGGESTED PARKING PLACE

W DRINKING-WATER TAP

BUILDINGS OR BUILT-UP AREA

+ CHURCH

YHA ▲ YOUTH HOSTEL

TRIANGULATION PILLAR

Introduction

The Ridgeway – 'greatest, lengthiest and noblest in appearance of all the prehistoric roads' – rides the back of one of the six great ridges that radiate from the central hub of Salisbury Plain. It sails the undulating waves of chalk downland through Wiltshire, Oxfordshire and Berkshire to the Thames Valley at Goring. This is open, airy country with breathtaking views across the vale. The way is not wild and barren – as might be supposed from a glance at the map – but punctuated with hedges and small woodlands and homely crops in large fields. Having descended to river level at Goring the ridge reaffirms itself in the north-easterly thrust of the Chiltern escarpment. But the contrast is striking: the escarpment is generously clothed in fine beechwoods and indented at near regular intervals with 'gaps' – natural valleys (and one unnatural, in the case of the M40 motorway through Beacon Hill) carrying important road and rail links. The fields are smaller, the footpaths more numerous, the human population more evident.

Keeping company with the Ridgeway, but at a lower level, is another ancient highway: the Icknield Way. Much of this is a highway in the strictly modern sense, where the interest is not in the walking but in the delightful villages along the way. From Watlington in Oxfordshire to as far north-east as Ivinghoe in Buckinghamshire it divides into the Upper and Lower Icknield Ways. The Lower way coincides with the B4009 and other roads over much of its length, while the Upper Way is a trackway running along the foot of the escarpment.

The Ridgeway Path, which runs from Ivinghoe Beacon in Buckinghamshire to Overton Hill in Wiltshire, should not be confused with the 'true' Ridgeway – at least not all of the time. The Path, proposed by the Ramblers Association as long ago as 1942 and brought into being by the Countryside Commission as part of a countrywide network of long-distance routes, follows the Icknield Way for 8 miles from Wainhill near Chinnor to a point one mile north of Swyncombe. Numerous meanderings here and there on well-known paths make up the total Chiltern contribution to the Ridgeway Path. West of Goring the Path follows the true Ridgeway along much of its length, the main exception being a few miles on low land between Liddington Hill and Barbury Castle in Wiltshire, where the Path instead sweeps south around Ogbourne St George on its way to the Marlborough Downs.

The Chiltern Hills and the Downland of Berkshire, Oxfordshire and Wiltshire are vestiges of a landscape of vast domes and ridges formed about 25 million years ago, when lateral forces distorted the earth's crust. The upper strata of these domes and ridges consist of great depths of chalk – many hundreds of feet in places – laid down in the sea 60 million years and more ago. In many places the chalk is overlaid by what are called 'superficial deposits of clay-with-flints'. The flints were formed within the chalk mass itself but the chalk has since dissolved away through the agency of percolating rainwater, leaving the flints suspended in a less soluble clay residue.

Prominent features of the Downs, particularly in the region between Marlborough and Avebury in Wiltshire, are the sarsen stones. Otherwise known as bridlestones, Druid stones or greywethers these hard, shapeless stones are scattered over a wide area. They are remnants of a one-time overlying stratum of hard sandstone which has been removed by weathering.

The flints, the sarsens, the chalk: each has played its part in the history of downland man. Flints in the manufacture of primitive weapons and tools, and, over more recent centuries, the construction of buildings and boundary walls; sarsens in the prehistoric stone circles of Avebury and Stonehenge; chalk rock in church and cottage walls.

It is thought that the Ridgeway is the oldest existing road in the world. It runs where we would expect the earliest roads to run: along the dry ridge-top where the going was relatively easy, rather than the marshy, densely-wooded vale. The Icknield Way, which came into being later, was clearly a useful compromise between the exposed ridge-top and the marshy vale below: it passes just above the 'spring-line' – that is above the contour where water issues from the base of the chalk. The Lower Icknield Way between Dunstable and Watlington may have been used more by wheeled traffic as this developed.

Throughout historic and prehistoric times the old roads were tramped by all manner of men: cattle drovers, local inhabitants on short journeys between adjacent settlements, long-distance travellers on pilgrimage to the ceremonial centres of Avebury and Stonehenge, and the less desirable marauders and plunderers. With all this activity we are not surprised to see numerous reminders of human occupation along the Ridgeway Path.

Most notable are the Iron Age forts (otherwise known as castles or camps), many of which are situated at strategic points overlooking the vale. Among the best known forts on, or close to, the Path are at Ivinghoe Beacon, Boddington Hill (overlooking Wendover), Pulpit Hill, Segsbury Down (above Wantage), Whitehorse Hill, Swinley Down (Alfred's Castle), Liddington Hill, Marlborough Downs (Barbury Castle). In general all you will see at these sites is a single rampart and ditch enclosing a large area of land.

Five hill figures accompany the route of the Ridgeway Path. They are cut into the thin turf – exposing the chalk – and are seen from considerable distances. Along the Chiltern section there is Whiteleaf Cross above Princes Risborough, Bledlow Cross above Chinnor and the White Mark above Watlington. In Oxfordshire the magnificent White Horse of Uffington overlooks the Vale of the White Horse; in Wiltshire the Hackpen Horse lies along the west-facing slope of the Marlborough Downs. At many places along the Path you will see sections of the extensive bank and ditch known as Grim's Ditch or Dyke, sweeping 'like a green bridge' across country. Opinions differ about the age and purpose of the dyke: Iron Age, Roman, Saxon, civil boundary or defensive rampart.

There seem to be more reminders of the death of prehistoric man than the activities of his life. His burial mounds or barrows (marked as 'tumuli' on the Ordnance Survey map) are scattered over a wide area. Long barrows belong to the Neolithic period (New Stone Age) while round barrows are usually of the Bronze Age. The round barrow is classified as either bowl, bell, disc, pond or saucer depending on its shape. The last few miles of the Path pass an area of particular interest; an area that was a centre of intensive human occupation during Neolithic times. Here is the stone circle of Avebury, the massive mound of Silbury Hill and the West Kennett Long Barrow – all within walking distance of the 'end' of the Ridgeway Path.

I have divided the guide into 14 walks, which in most cases start and finish at towns or villages lying on, or close to, the Path. In this way the complete Ridgeway Path is covered. Where possible I have given directions for circular routes so that you can return to the

11

starting point at the end of the day. Some of these routes are along footpaths or quiet roads; some make use of the best bus services; some are a combination of the two. In this way much of the Ridgeway Path can be traversed in relatively convenient and easy stages.

The official length of the Ridgeway Path is 85 miles (137km), but if you add to this all the return walking you have something like 125 miles (201km) in prospect. The Path throughout its entire length is marked by signposts, concrete plinths and white-painted acorn symbols. The Chiltern Society has done a marvellous job in waymarking footpaths in their area; you will find their white arrows a great help as you make your way along the return paths. Four 1:50,000 series Ordnance Survey maps cover the entire route – as well as the return paths: these are sheets 165, 173, 174 and 175. If you are fortunate enough to get hold of the earlier one-inch series you will need only three sheets: 157, 158 and 159.

After heavy rain much of the Path can be very muddy, especially along parts of the Oxfordshire and Wiltshire Downs. Good footwear is essential. Even wellingtons would not be out of place!

The bracketed numbers that you will find throughout the text are for the benefit of those who will be walking two or more sections in one go. For example, when walking from Ivinghoe Beacon to Wendover (i.e. without stopping-off at Tring), you will be redirected from a point near the end of the first chapter to the text following the '(1)' in the second chapter, thus avoiding the linking path to Tring. This arrangement gets a little complex on the Ridgeway above Wantage, but if you keep strictly to the numerical sequence all should be well.

Bus services are far from ideal and you are well advised to lay your hands on all available timetables (more details in the appendix); you can then make the most of the very limited services. When your 'return to base' depends on a bus ride it would be sensible to get part of the round trip out of the way before starting the walk. In other words: leave your car (or train, or whatever) at the 'end' of the walk and take the bus to the 'start'. Your car (or train!) will be there waiting for you at the end of the walk. I will leave you to work out all the variations on this theme, in particular where the return journey is partly on foot and partly by bus.

Depending on your means, accommodation may be less of a problem than transport. There are three well-placed youth hostels: Ivinghoe, Streatley, and Court Hill (on the downs above Wantage). Bradenham hostel, 4½ miles south of Princes Risborough, is not so well placed but can be reached by bus (a very infrequent bus!) Bed and breakfast accommodation close to the route is plentiful and a selection of addresses is given in the Appendix. A valuable compendium on all matters relating to the Ridgeway Path is the Ridgeway Information and Accommodation Guide. This is available from The Ridgeway Officer, Oxfordshire County Council, Speedwell House, Speedwell Street, Oxford OX1 1SD, and from tourist information centres.

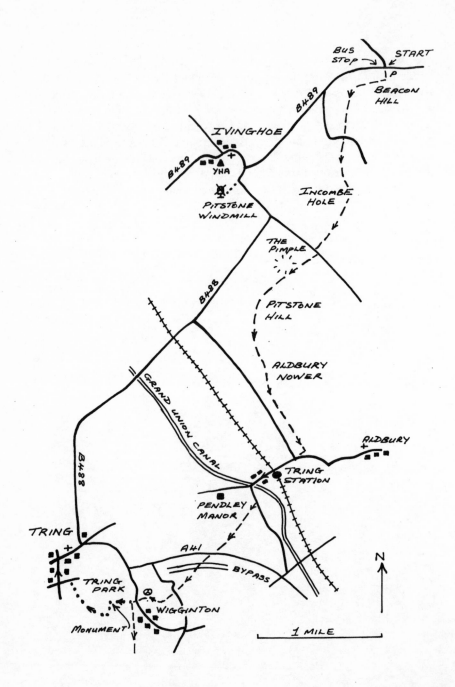

Ivinghoe Beacon to Tring

Introduction: As if to make the very best impression on us, the Ridgeway Path commences its 85 mile journey at Ivinghoe Beacon on the exhilarating summit of Beacon Hill. After crossing the open downland of Steps Hill and Pitstone Hill to lovely Aldbury Nower Wood, the Path descends to Tring Station and the Grand Union Canal in the Bulbourne Valley. At Wigginton – where the Ridgeway Path heads off to Hastoe and Wendover – we leave the official route and go down through the wooded park to Tring itself.

Distance: 6 miles (9.7km) including the descent through Tring Park.

Return: By bus to Ivinghoe Beacon.

Parking: There is a lay-by below Beacon Hill at the junction of the B489 with the Ivinghoe Aston Road 1¼ miles from Ivinghoe village (grid reference 963172).

The Walk: The best point from which to ascend Beacon Hill is from the lay-by mentioned above. A few steps from the lay-by, in the direction of Ivinghoe, a footpath sign directs you uphill through thorn bushes towards the Beacon. The path soon runs up alongside a wire fence bordering a field on the left. At the top of the path (there is a stile in the fence on the left) turn right and go along to the summit. An Ordnance Survey plinth stands at the top; also the mound of a bowl barrow. Having taken in the magnificent view, (which includes Whipsnade Zoo's white lion cut into the hillside) you should turn left through the middle of the barrow (or better still, around it!) and

15

descend the hill along a choice of paths all the way down to a road. On the way you will have crossed the faintly visible rampart of an Iron Age fort that surrounded the hill; you will see it clearly later as a notch in the hillside. The second small hill on the right is capped by a bowl barrow.

Cross the road to a wide path – to the right of a double ditch and opposite an old chained-off parking area. A short distance along the path a stone direction indicator beckons you off to the right. (You could go straight on uphill if you wish, but this may lead you into a very muddy experience – and the view isn't so good!) The correct path runs through the grass on the right and crosses two ditches before meeting a stile. It then goes slightly left to a waymark post under hawthorn trees. Don't go under the trees but stay on open ground, just following the trees as they curve left and uphill. A gap in the trees reveals a cattle trough. Go up past this and cross the grassland alongside the edge of a deep coombe. This will lead you to the second of two stiles ahead.

You are now (or should be!) back on that wide path, with the coombe, Incombe Hole, still on your right. Some 474 acres of land hereabouts is classified as a Site of Special Scientific Interest – partly because of the chalk grassland.

The path curves right and runs downhill to a stile leading into a field. Follow the path straight on across the field for ⅓ mile to the Aldbury-Ivinghoe road. Turn left in this and right after 75 yards into the top end of a small car park. Go over a stile and all the way up the broad slope of Pitstone Hill (see Historical Notes) – with a wire fence on your left. The rounded hill on your right is appropriately named 'The Pimple'. It makes an interesting diversion – especially for the children. The view from The Pimple takes in the cement works and chalk-pits, Ivinghoe village, Pitstone Windmill, and the distant waters of Tring reservoirs. The reservoirs, in addition to feeding the summit of the Grand Union Canal, are well known for their bird life.

Continue following the fence as it curves left over the hill, and when you are fairly close to a wood ahead, bear right – downhill – to a stile leading into the wood (Aldbury Nower). The path now follows the line of Grim's Dyke, firstly under a stand of beech trees and then deeper into the wood ahead. After about ¼ mile a flight of steps takes the woodland path down to a clearing. Follow the level path forward across the clearing and re-enter the wood. Another, longer flight of steps will then take you down to a crossing-track; turn right here and follow the track as it curves left and downhill. At the point where the track bears right and continues downhill under chestnut trees (to a road) you must turn left along a path that follows the top left-hand border of a field (with small trees and scrub to your left). Continue along this path until you pass a new building (Westland Farm) on your right. There are large beech trees lining the path at this point. Immediately after the trees you should turn right at a gate and go down to join the farm drive and a road.

You should normally turn right in the road but, if you have time to spare, I recommend that you turn left and walk the mile to the village of Aldbury. The village, with its delightful cottages, ancient stocks and village pond, lies at the foot of the wooded slopes of Aldbury Common. Good tea can be had at one of the cottages, so it is worth going that extra mile!

Now back to Westland Farm: on leaving the drive go down the road to Tring Station and the Grand Union Canal (see Historical Notes). After crossing the canal, turn left immediately and follow the road for 120 yards to an iron gate on the right. Strike across the field (between fences) to the near left-hand corner of a wood. The wood borders Pendley Manor, which is used as a College of Adult Education. An old record states that Pendley was 'a great town' in the 15th-century and that there were in the town '13 plows besides divers handicraft men'. In 1448 Sir Robert Wittingham of Pendley Manor razed the town, ploughed up the land and laid it down to pasture. Follow the wood-edge all the way to the A41.

Turn right and go along the A41 for about 75 yards. Cross to a stile opposite and follow an iron fence uphill – crossing the unfinished end of a bypass. (If the bypass is complete at the time of your arrival you will need to cross by the footbridge provided.) As you approach some beech trees near the top of the hill, a stile in the iron fence on the left will lead you into the corner of a large field. Follow the field's right-hand edge uphill to a stile in its far right-hand corner. This connects you to a lane. Turn right and cross to a stile on the left, then along a path between fences. The path soon turns right, leading you into a field. Follow the right-hand edge of the field (two fields, in fact), to a stile in its far right-hand corner. More parallel fences follow, then an Ordnance Survey plinth, then the road at Wigginton. Cross the road to a short drive opposite. The drive serves some houses on the left and ends at the entrance to Tring Park. We now leave the Ridgeway Path and go down through Tring Park to Tring itself. To continue on the Path, turn to (1) on page 22.

Henry Guy enclosed the park after Tring Manor was granted to him by Charles II. The enclosure met with much opposition from the 'poor of the parish'. In 1950 Alison Uttley wrote: 'Will Tring keep its supreme beauty, which is the Park? . . . no park that ever I saw excels it.' Tring Bypass now thrusts its rude course through this fine place. Go through the gate into the wood. At the first crossing path go slightly right (NOT slightly left!) and downhill to a junction of paths at an obelisk. This was erected in memory of Charles II's mistress Nell Gwynne (or her dog). Tradition has it that 'pretty, witty Nell' had a house here in the park.

Turn left at the obelisk into the downhill path; this leads to an iron gate and stile where the wood begins to clear. Turn right here and go downhill across the open park into a shallow valley; then straight on to cross the bypass over a footbridge. The impressive mansion ahead of you retains little of the house designed by Sir Christopher Wren for Henry Guy. This was enclosed within a much larger building following the purchase of the Manor by Baron Lionel Rothschild in 1872. It is now an Arts Education Trust school. Having crossed the bypass go along the tarmac path to Park Street. Turn left for Tring Zoological Museum. This houses an outstanding collection of specimens including mammals, birds, reptiles and fishes. It is now just a short walk along Akeman Street to the town centre.

Returning to Ivinghoe and Beacon Hill: Bus 61 from the Rose and Crown, Tring; two-hourly service every day (Sunday – p.m. only).

Historical Notes

Ivinghoe: In the village centre the imposing 18th-century Old Brewery House serves as the youth hostel; and the Old Town Hall next door is the public library. Cathedral-like St. Mary's church stands close by. Although it 'suffered some outrage' in 1871 in the name of 'restoration', there remains much to delight the eye – in particular the fine

15th-century roof. An enormous thatch-hook is attached to the churchyard wall. This was used to drag thatch from cottage roofs to prevent the spread of fire. Nearby Vicarage Lane has some charming old cottages – and the Rose and Crown pub.

Pitstone Windmill stands in a field ¼ mile south of Ivinghoe, just off the B488 road. Built in 1627 (or so an inscription seems to indicate) it is probably the oldest remaining windmill in England. In 1902, only 7 years after extensive repairs were carried out, a freak storm badly damaged the mill. It was not worked again commercially and remained derelict until 1937 when it was offered to the National Trust. Some repairs were put in hand at that time but complete restoration was not started until 1963.

Pitstone Hill: There is much archaeological interest here on Pitstone Hill. On the slope of the hill, in the general direction of the cement works, are the pits of old – probably neolithic – flint workings. There is also evidence of an Iron Age settlement and field system, a Roman well, a pagan Saxon burial site, and a section of Grim's Dyke. So it is not surprising that the hill has been designated a Site of Special Scientific Interest.

Tring Cutting: Tring station is at the southern end of this famous cutting. Built between 1834 and 1838 to carry the London-Birmingham line through the Chilterns, the cutting is 2½ miles long and 57 feet deep for a ¼ mile. The station itself was regarded as 'first class' and boasted 'one inspector, three policemen, four porters and one stationary-engine man'.

The Canal also has a deep cutting to take it through the Chiltern escarpment. This is 1½ miles long and was completed in 1797 as part of what was then known as the Grand Junction Canal. The 3 mile summit level of the canal extends in both directions from this crossing; it is fed with water from reservoirs near Marsworth. Many improvements have been made over the years in an effort to increase the amount of available water, but this has resulted in a very complex system. The British Waterways Board have renovated this stretch of the canal – from Northchurch to Marsworth – with the object of promoting public and government interest in the national canal network.

Tring: The town was once an important centre for lace and straw plait making, cottage industries now largely extinct. It also boasted a silk mill with the largest water wheel in Hertfordshire – 22 feet in diameter. The mill buildings can be seen in Brook Street.

Tring to Wendover

Introduction: Before meeting the Ridgeway Path at Wigginton, today's route crosses Tring Bypass and ascends the attractive wooded slope of Tring Park. The Path then runs along the border between Tring Park and Wigginton's back gardens. Beyond Wigginton lie Hastoe, Wendover Forest and Hale Woods. You may well enjoy the return walk along the Wendover canal every bit as much as the Ridgeway Path itself; but do carry binoculars – the canal is also enjoyed by kingfishers!

Distance: 7 miles (11.3km), including the one mile link from Tring to the Ridgeway Path.

Return: by bus all the way,
or: walk the Wendover Canal towpath for 3½ miles (5.6km), then 'bus' the remaining 2 miles,
or: walk the entire 6 miles (9.7km) along the canal path and other paths.

Parking in Tring: There's a large free car park off the High Street – not far from the Rose & Crown.

The Walk: The A41 road through Tring is met by Akeman Street 200 yards west of the church. Go along Akeman Street and turn left into Park Street alongside the Zoological Museum. At a tile-hung house 150 yards along Park Street turn right into a path signposted 'Tring Park and Wigginton'. This takes you between wire fences to the footbridge over Tring Bypass. Having crossed the bypass follow

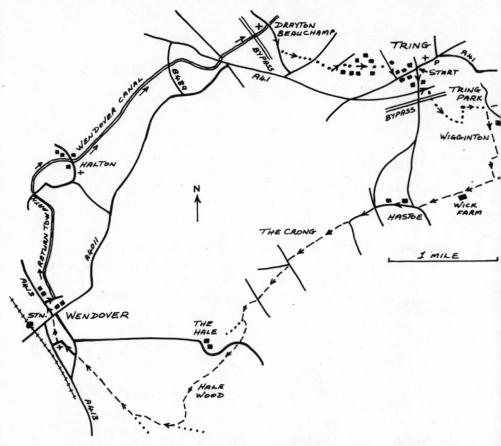

the left-hand edge of the field for a few yards – with the bypass on your left – and then bear half-right across the park towards the distant wooded slope. You will go down into a shallow valley and up alongside an old wire fence to meet the wood. The Mansion House is in view behind you.

Immediately you enter the wood turn left at a gate and stile and go uphill along a woodland drive to meet a junction of ways at Nell Gwynne's Obelisk. Here you must make a 90 degrees right turn (not acutely right) into a narrow uphill path. At the next crossing drive keep straight on along the level path which soon leads you to a gate. Turn right immediately along a narrow path running between a house and the wood.

(1) You are now on the Ridgeway Path and at the start of a long stretch that follows Wigginton's back gardens. A drive is crossed and

the path continues to follow the gardens. The path turns sharp right and soon runs into a field at a stile. Turn left and follow the field's left-hand border until you reach a track. Turn right in the track and follow it for ¾ mile – passing Wick Farm en route – to a road.

At a T-junction follow the road (Church Lane) signposted to Hastoe. You will pass Hastoe Cross Cottage on your right almost immediately. Where the road turns sharp left ¼ mile further on, go half-right into Pavis Wood and continue in roughly the same direction as before. This woodland path (a wide track at the start) is about ¾ mile long and for much of its length is not far from the left-hand extremity of the wood.

The path leaves the wood from its far left-hand corner at the summit of a steep narrow road. Turn left onto this and walk ahead for a few yards. Immediately after passing an aerial mast on your left, go half-right over a stile in the corner of a field. Cross the field diagonally (half-left) to a stile at the near right-hand corner of a small rectangular conifer plantation. Follow the right-hand edge of the plantation – which soon merges into a hedge – to a stile at a road.

Cross the road to a lane opposite and follow this into Wendover Woods. The wood is one of the Forestry Commission's many forest parks, with routes laid out for horse-riders and walkers. The highest point of the Chilterns is in this wood, the O.S. map showing a spot-height of 857 feet on the road just crossed. The path ahead leads you alongside beech trees. As it descends the hill and sinks between high banks, it is accompanied by woodland on each side. Now don't go blindly on all the way downhill! When a clearing appears on your left-hand side you should turn left, scramble out of the sunken path, and go uphill alongside the upper extremity of a large field.

Your view down-field includes a huddle of cottages and farm buildings at The Hale, set against the backcloth of Wendover Gap. Go right with the path at the top edge of the wood and stay with it until it ends at a narrow road. Go just a few steps downhill and join a wide path on the left which runs through Hale Wood.

After ¾ mile the track through Hale Wood turns half-left. You should go left with this, ignoring lesser-used paths going off right and left nearby. Turn right at a T-junction ahead and follow the path downhill. Ignore the path going off half-left after 150 yards and turn right after a further 75 yards. The narrow way-marked path on the left soon after this should also be ignored! Continue all the way downhill to meet a track at the bottom. Go ahead along this and turn right to meet Boswell's Farm opposite a fine avenue of beech trees. Stay in the track – which evolves into a lane and passes farm buildings on the left – for ½ mile to a crossroads. Boddington Hill is over to your right. Hidden among the trees on this spur of Wendover Woods is the site of an Iron Age fort.

Cross to Church Lane opposite and follow this to St. Mary's Church. The church is ½ mile from the centre of Wendover. The story goes that witches or fairies carried away the building materials from what would have been a site closer to Wendover. Inside there is a plaque commemorating one William Bradshawe, his wife, 9 children and 23 grandchildren – but you will have to take my word for it because the church, having suffered vandalism, is now open only during services.

Turn right into Heron Path, opposite the lych-gate of the church and follow it past a large pond and park on the left. The path passes Heron Cottage, turns left and runs alongside a stream to meet a lane. Cross the lane and go ahead to Wendover High Street.

Returning to Tring: Bus 28 direct to Tring (infrequent service, Mon-Sat only),
or: Bus 55/56/57 to Aylesbury (2 journeys per hour Mon-Sat; hourly Sun) then bus 61/x61 or 501 to Tring (½-hourly to hourly Mon-Sat; 2-hourly Sun). This is a long way round but provides an opportunity to visit Aylesbury.

Walking Back: From the clock tower go along Aylesbury Road (A413) to the first turning on the right – Wharf Road. A school sign in Wharf Road marks the start of the Wendover Canal and its accompanying towpath. The canal dates back to 1797 and linked Wendover with the Grand Union Canal near Marsworth. The first port of call is Halton village 1½ miles along the towpath. Halton's beautifully kept churchyard is worth at least a few minutes of your time. You may find the numerous gravestones to R.A.F. personnel (R.A.F. Halton is nearby) thought provoking, if not very moving.

Now you must ignore the footpath sign aimed at the left bank of the canal and cross a stile to the right bank, where an excellent towpath will take you all the way to the A41. I have seen kingfishers along this stretch: so do keep your eyes peeled!

You could now save yourself 2½ miles of walking by catching a bus into Tring. Otherwise: cross the A41 and walk along the left bank of the canal to where the water disappears into a concrete sump. Now you may choose to stay on the canal path as far as the next bridge (I will see you there later) or come with me over the stile on the left and contemplate the delightful precincts of Drayton Beauchamp church. I hope your visit here precedes the construction of Aston Clinton Bypass, which will cross the canal just here. The tranquillity of this place is to be thrust aside.

Once over that stile go half-right to another stile, and into a meadow. Rights of way abound here so I suggest you aim at the gate in the furthest corner of the meadow (unless you wish to visit the church, which is a Grade I Listed Building – and which may be locked!). The gate leads on to a drive, which you should follow to its T-junction with a road. Turn right in the road and go along to a canal bridge (where those who stayed on the canal path will have arrived). Then go uphill in the road and turn left into a drive just before the road itself turns left. You will pass a garage on the right, followed by kennels.

Proceed uphill to a gate and stile and straight on along a concrete drive towards a collection of low farm buildings (an old pig farm). Go slightly left to a stile and gate leading into a field, then work your way uphill to a waymarked stile at the top edge of the field. (Strictly speaking the right-of-way runs anticlockwise around the field-edge.) This will place you in another field, which you should cross half-left in the direction of two 'intensive' farm buildings. (Perhaps that's where the pigs have gone!) Pass to the left of these buildings, alongside a hedge to a stile, then to another stile at a road (The Upper Icknield Way).

Go a few steps left (I repeat *left*, not right!) in the road and cross to a stile opposite; then half-left across a meadow to a solitary beech tree backed by houses. Manipulate yourself over the stile here and go along the tarmac path on the other side for 30 yards and turn right between houses to a road. It's nearly all houses from now on. Turn left into Buckingham Road and go along this to a footpath on the right just after Ann's Close (which is on the left). You now have a succession of three paths running between houses and ending at a recreation ground. Another path takes you across the 'rec', passes a school and terminates at a road. Go right here and along to the A41; then turn left for Tring.

Historical Note:

Wendover: Robert Louis Stevenson's phrase 'a straggling, purposeless sort of place' is unlikely to gain a sympathetic hearing today. A busy place certainly, but straggling and purposeless – no! Those who find pleasure in old buildings will be delighted with it. For example, in the High Street there is the Swan and Brewers, the 17th-century Red Lion (where it is thought Cromwell and Stevenson stayed) and 16th-century Bosworth House. The Clock Tower at the lower end of High Street, dates back to 1842 and once housed a horse-drawn fire engine. It now houses an excellent tourist information centre. Thatched Coldharbour Cottages in Tring Road were apparently part of Henry VIII's dowry to Anne Boleyn. A sail-less windmill tower stands just off Aylesbury Road. The mill was first put into operation in 1804. The cap is said to be the largest in England and the tower one of the tallest. It is now a private house.

Wendover to Princes Risborough

Introduction: Now we have what is probably the most beautiful part of the Ridgeway Path. First the ascent of 842-ft Coombe Hill, popular with walkers, picnickers and kitefliers; then through fine beechwoods to the Chequers estate (the Prime Minister's country home) and alongside the nature reserve below Pulpit Hill. After climbing the steep wooded slope of Whiteleaf Hill to Whiteleaf Cross we descend to the pleasant town of Princes Risborough.

Distance: 6 miles (9.7km) of Ridgeway Path.

Return: The return route to Wendover consists of a short bus or train ride to Little Kimble followed by 3 miles (4.8km) easy walking, or a slightly longer bus ride to Butler's Cross followed by 2 miles (3.2km) walking.

Parking in Wendover: There are a number of official roadside slots in Tring Road (A4011), near the clock tower. You could also try Aylesbury Road (A413). The car park off High Street is short term only.

The Walk: From Wendover's Pound Street, which is the continuation of High Street, go over the railway bridge into Ellesborough Road (the B4010). Then, passing some cottages on the right, go up to the sharp bend in the road. Leave the road here and join a path starting from the left-hand side. This divides into two immediately. Take the right-hand path uphill through the trees, ignoring further left and right-hand branches. There's a flight of steps to help you on your

27

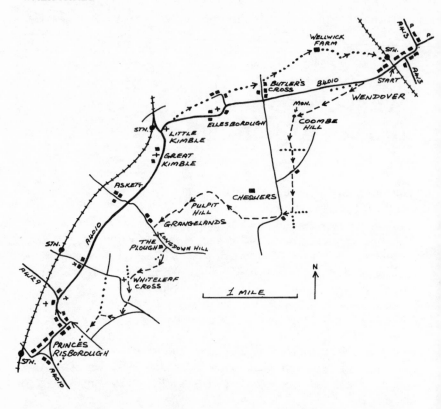

way, and a grassy ditch to guide you. This is good country for birds, wild-flowers, and blackberries!

Advancing uphill you will eventually reach the Boer War monument on the 842-ft summit of Coombe Hill. This is the highest viewpoint in the Chilterns (not to be confused with the highest *point,* which is 3 miles away in Wendover Woods). Here the chalk grassland, heath and woodland are included in a Site of Special Scientific Interest. I am told that St. Paul's Cathedral can be seen from this elevated position, but I have my doubts! Ellesborough Church is in view ¾ mile westward, overlooked by Beacon Hill. The church has the distinction of being attended by certain national leaders during their visits to nearby Chequers, the Prime Minister's country home. Chequers can be seen to the south-west; but more of that later.

Turn left at the monument and pass to the right of a line of gorse, thorn and oak, with the golf course down below on your right. Stay more or less at this level until you approach a wire fence running downhill. Don't go over the stile directly ahead, but bear left to another stile under trees higher up in the fence. Cross the stile into a beech wood and go straight ahead with a field just to your left. In less than ¼ mile you will arrive at a road with a flint cottage opposite.

Turn right in the road and go down for 100 yards to a rough drive on the left. When this soon turns left at an iron gate go right into a wood along a waymarked path. This is a large wood and you could easily go astray; so you must keep your eyes on those acorn signs as if your life depended on it! For about ½ mile they will lead you more-or-less straight on through the wood: firstly with a field on your left; eventually to join a sunken way. Soon after this they will steer you right at a crossing-track, and downhill. Then over another crossing-track and straight on – with fields right and left – to the road at Buckmoorend, which you will find overlooks the Chequers estate (see Historical Notes).

You should cross the road to the stile opposite and follow the clearly marked path across the estate. The road runs parallel on your left, and Chequers is in view on your right. You will cross the main drive about 100 yards from the lodge gates. This is known as Victory Drive and was planted with beech trees by Sir Winston Churchill. The path then crosses a field uphill to a stile at the left-hand corner of a wood. It turns right here and follows the edge of the wood for about ⅓ mile to a stile on the left. Now you must be careful: cross the stile and strike across the centre of the next field keeping the woods on your left – and right-hand at equal distances – for the first few yards at least. Go forward along the rising path to a stile adjacent to an iron gate, and straight on to the head of a deep coombe.

The coombe has the delightful name Happy Valley and is part of a BBONT nature reserve and a Site of Special Scientific Interest. While it is a haven for an interesting collection of plants and animals its primary distinction is that it is thought to be one of only three natural boxwoods in England. After passing the coombe the path divides two ways; take the uppermost branch, which cuts across a ditch. There are a number of these 'linear ditches' hereabouts; their origins are uncertain, but it is likely they are associated with the Iron

29

Age fort on Pulpit Hill.

A small rounded hill called Chequers Knap lies ahead of you; go past the left-hand side of this to a stile under trees. Then go downhill along a sunken path for a few yards and turn half-left into a short path to a stile. Now go straight ahead – with the butts of an old firing range on your left – to join the remnants of an old wire fence below a beech wood. The wood clothes Pulpit Hill, which is itself crowned by the Iron Age fort mentioned earlier. Go over a stile in the far left-hand corner of this piece of open scrubland. Continue in the same direction – but don't go dashing on! (although at some future date you may be directed to do just that – all the way to Longdown Hill.) Turn right very soon – beside a notice for horseriders – and left after 15 yards through a gap in the hedge. A short path will usher you into a field.

The area of scrub and grassland over to your left is known as Grangelands and is another Nature Reserve managed by BBONT. Grangelands is freely open to the public and is noted for its rich variety of wild flowers, butterflies and birds. Strike across the field in the direction of a coniferous wood at the far end. The path enters the wood at mid-point (of the field) and plunges steeply between wire fences to a road (Longdown Hill). Turn left in the road and follow this up to a side road (Cadsden Road) in which stands The Plough.

Turn right into a bridleway immediately beyond The Plough. After 25 yards you must leave the bridleway at a stile and gate by turning half left into a beech wood. The woodland path soon divides two ways; take the right-hand branch (the steepest) and go uphill along what becomes – near the summit – a very steep climb. This is Whiteleaf Hill.

At the summit the trees give way and you can look down on Princes Risborough. The green heights of Wainhill occupy the middle distance while the thin hazy line of the Oxfordshire Downs projects along the horizon. Directly in front of you and almost hidden from view on the steep downward slope, is Whiteleaf Cross, carved out of the chalk. As with many other hill figures, the Cross is steeped in mystery and controversy. Of the many theories propounded, the one I prefer (illogically, perhaps) states that the pyramid base was cut by prehistoric man as a landmark for the traveller and the Cross added as a devotional symbol in Christian times.

At the top of the hill, just above the Cross and to one side, a small group of ash trees marks the site of a Neolithic barrow. This was excavated in the 1930s by Sir Lindsay Scott. A timber burial chamber and the scattered remains of a middle-aged man were found here; also numerous flint instruments and fragments of pottery, on which impressions of cultivated cereal grains were found. Another, smaller, mound can be seen a short distance northwards beside a grassy path. This one has a cross impressed upon it and may be the site of a former windmill (a refreshing change from burial mounds!).

Standing with the Cross in front of you, you should turn left and go along the level path through the woods (ignoring two right-hand branches) to a car park and picnic area. Drop down to the road here, turn right and go along the road for a few yards to a concrete drive going off to the left and uphill. At the top of the slope follow the drive round to the left until it comes to an abrupt end. Keeping the woods to your left, go ahead to a stile and forward between the woods and a single line of trees. Then bear right to a stile at a road.

Now *don't* go into the road but make a 90 degrees right-hand turn to cross the open hillside in the general direction of Princes Risborough. If you have judged that 90 degrees turn correctly and have not followed the downward road too closely, you will meet a stile lower down on the slope of the hill. From here a path will take you all the way down to a track – the Upper Icknield Way; and the steeple of Princes Risborough Church will be directly ahead. Turn left in the Way and go with it until it meets a road. To continue on the Ridgeway Path turn to (2) on page 35; or turn right in the road for Princes Risborough.

Returning to Wendover: The 323/324 bus from Princes Risborough Market Square is half-hourly, Sundays 2-hourly. The 323 will take you to Little Kimble Church – but not on Sundays, the 324 to Butler's Cross. Railway buffs could go by train to Little Kimble Station: 1-3 hour service, not Sundays.

If Butler's Cross is your destination, start from (*) below.

From the bus stop at Little Kimble go along Ellesborough Road (B4010) to All Saints Church, (if you have arrived by train you should turn right when leaving the station and left into Ellesborough Road). The church is well known for its 13th-Century wall paintings and tiles.

Ignore the first footpath on the left as the road curves right and continue along to the second. This starts beside the 'Ellesborough' sign, just beyond Swanland House. The path runs alongside houses and gardens before entering open fields, from where you will have a good view of Ellesborough Church. Go straight on (aiming slightly right of two white-painted houses) across two fields in succession. A stile under a hawthorn tree marks the termination of the second field. Continue forward across the next (narrow) field, passing a shed on the right, to a gate.

The gate leads you into a lane and alongside an attractive cottage. When the lane turns right go forward along a path bordering the left-hand side of a bungalow ('The Bothy'), then straight on across a field to a stile (more bungalows in view ahead). Cross the next field along a narrow path between fences, to the road at Butler's Cross. Turn left in the road (or right to the post office for cream teas and other goodies!) and cross over to a stile after 40 yards.

(*)Those who have arrived here by bus should disembark at the post office and walk away from the main road to the stile on the right. This is beyond the last house (no. 7).

Go over that stile and forward to another stile (and gate) leading into a wide track. When the track soon runs into a right-hand field go ever so slightly left, then forward again along the right-hand edge of a field to a stile in its far right-hand corner. Then forward again, with a wire fence on your left, to another stile. Strike across the next field in the direction of a small copse. Two stiles more and you are alongside an orchard; a third stile leads you out into the field ahead. As you pass the boundary fence of a tall Elizabethan farmhouse on the right (Wellwick Farm – a Grade I Listed Building) you should steer half-right to a stile and gate in a farm drive. Go forward to a T-junction in the drive (passing barns on the right) and step into the field ahead. Turn left immediately and follow the fenced edge of the field until you reach a telephone pole approximately opposite the first of two farm houses (these are on the far side of the drive). Now you must concentrate!

Turn right at the pole and follow the path across a large field. If in doubt aim roughly towards the break in the hills. The path curves left and, later, right to join a stile in a hedge-gap. Go over this stile and follow the left-hand edge of a field. The tree stumps in the hedge bear witness to a magnificent line of elms that graced this field in earlier days. Aim for the stile slightly right of the field's far left-hand corner. Once over this go right a few paces, then half-left across a field in the direction of Wendover railway station's footbridge. Before you reach the footbridge you will have a cricket pitch to circumnavigate by following its boundary hedges first right, then left.

Historical Notes

Chequers: The house has been much altered and enlarged since its original construction, which was probably in the 1560s. It was given to the nation by Lord Lee of Fareham in 1917 to be used as a retreat for the Prime Minister. David Lloyd George was the first to take up residence, but he – like his successor Bonar Law – did not altogether welcome the opportunity. Later Prime Ministers have shown more appreciation. Winston Churchill made good use of Chequers during his term of office in the Second World War; it was his 'power house of strategy'.

Princes Risborough: 'Untidy Metroland below the Chilterns' is how John Betjeman saw Princes Risborough. This may be true of the town as a whole but not (to my mind) of the confines of Church Street and High Street. The old Market House stands at the focal point of these two streets and is still used by stallholders on market day. 17th-century Cromwell House in Church Street has been rescued from a state of dilapidation and restored by Buckinghamshire County Council. This has earned it a Scheme of Merit placing in the European Architectural Heritage Year awards. The red-brick Mansion House opposite the church is in the care of the National Trust. Part of the house may be viewed by the public – but by written appointment only.

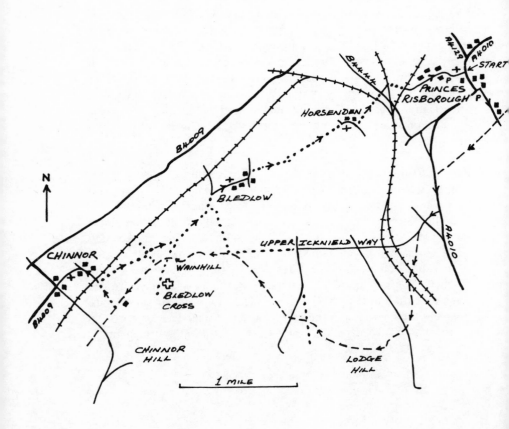

Princes Risborough to Chinnor

Introduction: After meandering along pleasant paths in the Risborough Gap and over Lodge Hill to Hempton Wainhill the Ridgeway Path follows the Upper Icknield Way for 6 straight miles. We leave the Way after only one of these miles and return to Princes Risborough via Chinnor and the attractive villages of Bledlow and Horsenden. Lodge Hill is worth every step – as are Wainhill and Bledlow – places to return to again and again!

Distance: 5½ miles (8.8km) including the ½ mile link from the Ridgeway Path to Chinnor.

Return: 3½ miles (5.6km) easy walking (no bus I'm afraid!).

Parking in Princes Risborough: There are two good car parks: one in Horns Lane where the walk starts (short-term except on Sundays), the other near the church (approach from Church Street).

The Walk: From Princes Risborough High Street turn left into Horns Lane and then right into New Road. Follow New Road uphill for ⅓ mile and turn right into the clearly marked Upper Icknield Way (2). Go along the Way until you meet a main road (A4010). Turn left here and, after ½ mile, right into a narrow road (the Upper Icknield Way again) signposted to Bledlow. Go over a crossroad and, after passing a house on the left, into a field on the left through a wide gap in the hedge.

Now follow the right-hand edge of the field for half its length and go half-left across the field approximately midway between two elec-

35

tricity pylons. The path may not be obvious but if you head for a kissing gate at the extremity of the field you cannot go far wrong. You will then cross two separated railway lines, each with its complement of kissing gates. From the last gate go along the left-hand edge of a field to a stile, then on through the next field to two stiles near its far left-hand corner. There are small electricity pylons nearby. The stiles will lead you into a field, then alongside a house at the centre of the field, and onto a road.

Cross the road to a field opposite and go along its left-hand edge to the far left-hand corner. Lodge Hill is directly ahead (or should be!). Go through a gap in the hedge and uphill to a stile – a convenient place to rest and to contemplate the view back across the valley. On the summit of a ridge opposite you will see Lacey Green Windmill. This has been lovingly restored by the Chiltern Society and now relives its former glory. Princes Risborough lies below the north-western extremity of the ridge, its church steeple clearly visible. Cut into the chalk on the hillside above the town is Whiteleaf Cross.

Having crossed the stile you should go half-right among scattered brambles across the slope of the hill. Princes Risborough will now be on your right. The path passes through a group of beech trees and out on to a grassy ridge. It then descends the hill among scrub and small trees and runs alongside a hedge. In the field on your right are two Bronze Age bell barrows. One is just discernible as a smoothly rounded mound quite close to the path. Excavation of these sites has revealed human bones, pottery fragments, finely worked flint saws and other flint implements. Follow the hedge as its passes between fields and go over a stile on the left. Cross a field to another stile, and on again to a road.

From the stile opposite go forward along the left-hand border of a field; then over a stile in the hedge a short distance before the field's far left-hand corner. Once over the stile you should keep more or less to the right-hand edge of the next field for about ¼ mile, heading for the far right-hand extremity of a large beech wood (Bledlow Great Wood). The exit from the field is at a stile close to an electricity power line.

The Upper Icknield Way is on the other side of the stile. We shall be following this to Watlington and beyond (but not all of it today!). Turn left after crossing the stile and follow the Icknield Way through the beech wood, ignoring a right-hand branch (to Bledlow). You will soon pass a timber cottage on your right, and, ¼ mile further on, a cottage on your left at a footpath 'junction'. The path going uphill just beyond the cottage provides a rewarding diversion since it leads to Chinnor Hill Nature Reserve and to the Bledlow Cross. Staying in the level track you will shortly see a gap in the trees on the left: a very nice place for lunch – with a picnic table provided by BBONT (Berkshire, Buckinghamshire and Oxfordshire Naturalists Trust)! When you pass two houses on the left, followed by a tennis court, this is your signal to turn right and go down a track to Chinnor – unless you are continuing on the Ridgeway Path, in which case read from (3) on page 39.

Returning to Princes Risborough: Retrace your steps along Keens Lane and, soon after crossing a railway line go left at a Y-junction. A stile then leads you along a level path across fields. This path eventually turns left alongside a timber fence to meet a stile and then a drive. Turn right in the drive for a few yards and go over a stile on the left – just before 'Pixies Nest'! (There is a post box just here.) Now you may find the next piece a little tricky: you should pass to the right of a small hay barn – to a stile; then ½-right into a right-hand field. Follow the field's left-hand edge to a stile (or a gap) beside a cattle trough, then forward along the left-hand edge of the next field – marked by a line of newly-planted trees. Go over a stile in the far left-hand corner of the present field; then make your way very slightly right across the next field towards an iron gate leading onto a rough track. Turn left onto the track and follow it downhill until it curves right; then go straight on across a field to Bledlow.

Passing The Lions on your right (the only pub in England with 3 lions, apparently) go through the village along Church End. The church itself will soon appear on the left, followed by 'Lyde Garden'. The Lyde is a tiny river which emerges from the ground at a considerable depth and flows into a deep ravine. Before being landscaped and civilised it was a wild and fascinating place. Turn left at the T-junction ahead – into Perry Lane, and then go downhill to a rough drive on the right just before Forge Cottage.

You will encounter chalets and semi-dereliction before entering a field. Proceed along the right-hand edge of this and the next field.

From the far right-hand corner of the second field go left under scrub for 50 yards and then right into another field. Follow the left-hand hedge before launching forward into an open field, where you should pass to the right of a tall pylon. One short step over a stream and a longer one over a stile (in a hedge) will place you in a meadow. The gate on the far side of the meadow will lead you out past a large timber barn and onto a road. This is Horsenden. Passing the church on your right go along the road to a path on the left just beyond Gate Cottage. There is a post box here. Along the path you will cross 3 stiles in succession before entering the grounds of the Building Research Establishment. You will then pass under a railway bridge before meeting the B4444 road.

Cross to Summerleys Road opposite and go along this and under another railway bridge. Soon after the bridge turn ½-right across a field to a railway crossing (Princes Risborough is another Clapham Junction – or so it seems!). Beyond the crossing a short path between houses leads you into Mount Road. Turn left at the end of Mount Road and you will soon be back in Princes Risborough.

Historical Notes

Chinnor Hill Nature Reserve: This has the reputation of being an 'ecological close-up of the social history of the Earth's vegetative life', which to most of us means that it is a delightful place through which to walk and enjoy the natural world. It is the property of the Berkshire, Buckinghamshire and Oxfordshire Naturalists' Trust (BBONT) who have kindly allowed the public free access on foot.

Bledlow Cross: This is a large figure cut into the chalk on Chinnor Hill. It can be reached by going up the Nature Reserve path for about 200 yards and scrambling up the very steep left bank at a point where the ground has been severely razed (by previous visitors!). It is thought by some commentators that the Cross dates back to the Middle Ages. Others consider it to be no more than 300 years old. Those are the dull facts (or fallacies!). On the lighter side a saying goes that if you run up and down and across it your strength will be renewed: a timely note for the faint-hearted.

Chinnor to Watlington

Introduction: We now follow six more straight and level miles of the Upper Icknield Way, much of it overlooked by the fine beech-clad slopes of the Chiltern Escarpment. But for the intrusive M40, which crosses the Way below Beacon Hill, this is a very pleasant walk, and not too demanding. Watlington is an attractive and useful place to call a halt, with its old buildings, its shops and its eating houses. It is also an ideal place to gather strength for the return journey, which is through Pyrton and along the Lower Icknield Way.

Distance: 7 miles (11.3km), including two ½ mile links with the Ridgeway Path – one at each end of the walk.

Return: 7½ level miles (12.1km).

Parking in Chinnor: Cars can be left alongside St. Andrew's Church or in front of the shops nearby. Plans are afoot for a public car park off Keens Lane, in what is now a field.

The Walk: From St. Andrew's Church, go along to the shopping parade and turn right into Keens Lane. Stay in the lane as it curves left opposite the Post Office. You will cross a railway line (see Historical Notes) before meeting a Y-junction in what is now a track. Fork right at the Y-junction and head up towards the hills. When you have sight of a tennis court (here of all places!) turn right into a wide track – the Upper Icknield Way. (3)The Chinnor Road is soon crossed, then after 1½ miles, the Kingston Blount Road. The house just here was the crossing keeper's cottage for the old Princes Risborough –

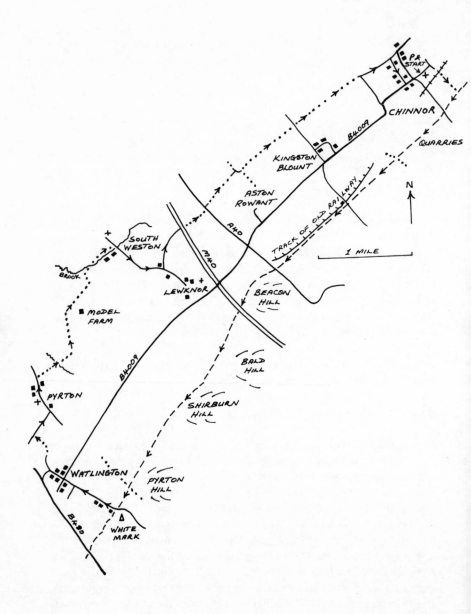

Watlington railway. Much of the overgrown track-bed can still be seen where it runs alongside the Ridgeway Path.

Another mile and you are at the A40 Stokenchurch-Oxford Road (where accommodation is provided at Beacon Cottage). Go straight on from here and follow the track along the lower slope of Beacon Hill. The small beech wood on your right is Lewknor Copse; this is leased by BBONT from All Souls College in order to preserve the spurge laurel and the rare white and narrow-lipped helleborines. Aston Rowant Nature reserve lies directly opposite Lewknor Copse. Quoting from the nature trail leaflet, 'The Reserve of approximately 300 acres was established in 1958 to conserve a fine example of chalk downland with a rich variety of plant life . . .'.

After suffering the indignity of a concrete M40 tunnel (see Historical Notes) the Path crosses delightful open country below Bald Hill. (Bald indeed but for a thin line of trees!) Now keep to the straight track for 2 miles or so to the Watlington Road (B480). A bungalow (No. 90) marks the spot. On the way you will have gone under a lovely canopy of sycamore, ash and beech and over two crossing tracks. Turn right along the road for Watlington. To continue on the Path turn to (4) on page 45.

The pyramid-shaped White Mark cut into the chalk on Watlington Hill (best seen from lower down the road) has been likened to a 'ghostly shadow of a church spire lying along the hill'. It was cut in 1764 under the direction of Edward Horne of Greenfield. Why, I can only guess!

Returning to Chinnor: From the war memorial in Watlington High Street go along Chapel Street (to the right of Cross Cottage) and follow it round to the right – passing the Chequers Pub. When the road turns right opposite a school, go left along a tarmac path, with the school fence on the left and allotments on the right. Stay with the path when it turns left beyond the school and follows the left-hand edge of a field. Turn right in the road ahead, then left at a T-junction ahead. Follow the road as it bears right opposite Pyrton Church. Leave the road just beyond The Plough and join a track on the right – next to 'The Old Forge'. After passing a metal barn go to the left of a gatehouse along a track. Follow this to an iron gate and stile just before a stream and straight on until you are within a long stone's throw of a house ahead. The 'Private' notice should stop you venturing too close!

Now cross a stile on the left waymarked 'OW'. This is a piece of the Oxfordshire Way which runs from Henley in Surrey to Bourton-on-the-Water in Gloucestershire, and serves our purpose very nicely! With your back to the stile aim almost ½-right to the far right-hand corner of the field (or the near-end of a thin line of tall trees). On arrival, cross a stile (ignoring a farm track right) and continue in the same direction across another field, aiming for the far right-hand corner again. A stile here will place you on a farm drive. Cross to another stile opposite and proceed along the left-hand edge of a field – under tall trees – to a stile in the far left-hand corner. Then go left and (immediately) right to resume the original direction, but now along the right-hand edge of a large field. The right-of-way in this field runs anticlockwise around the field-edge to a waymark post in the furthest corner.The waymark well to the left of this (under an oak tree) should be ignored!

Cross a stile in that corner and turn right immediately to another after 15 yards. Go left after the second stile and follow the left-hand edge of a field to a footbridge over a stream. Turn right after crossing the footbridge and follow the right-hand edge of a field, alongside a stream, until you link up with a drive at South Weston (after passing a 'Capability Brown' establishment on the right!)

Turn right at a T-junction ahead and, after passing a magnificent flint and brick farmhouse on the left, go along the road for ½ mile to a large house (Moor Court) on the left. Turn left into a lane soon after this (opposite 'The Manor'). The lane passes under the M40 and then meets the A40. Go left for 30 yards along the A40 and cross to the Lower Icknield Way opposite. Turn right at a T-junction in the Way after ½ mile; then left after 30 yards to resume your previous direction. Chinnor is now 2½ miles off and will be coming into view after the Kingston Blount road is crossed. For a quiet return to St. Andrew's Church turn right into Cherry Tree Road – after passing a school on the left. A short path links the end of this road to the B4009, where a left turn will take you back to the church.

Historical Notes

The Princes Risborough to Watlington Railway: This was opened in 1872 over its 8½ mile length and was run by a small private company until 1883; it was then purchased for £23,000 by the G.W.R. The Chinnor-Princes Risborough section of the line serves the Chinnor cement works and remains intact.

The M40: A motorway anywhere in the Chilterns is bound to be a disaster, but especially so here. The impact of this incursion on the Chiltern skyline would have been lessened if the Minister of Transport of an earlier day had not flown in the face of all opposition and decided on the present route. An alternative route, put forward by the two internationally respected experts Ove Arup and Geoffrey Jellicoe and all the amenity societies, was to have cut through woodland on the north-east side of the A40 with a less damaging effect on this beautiful stretch of downland. The motorway has inflicted irreparable damage to the Aston Rowant Nature Reserve through which it passes.

Watlington: You will find Watlington a delightful place, particularly when you explore the High Street beyond the confines of the 17th-century town hall. The High Street itself leads you to lesser streets and pathways where it is a pleasure to walk. Watlington can claim an important place in history in at least one respect: it was here that the anti-Royalist John Hampden spent the night before being fatally wounded at the Battle of Chalgrove Field on 18th June 1643. He died six days later.

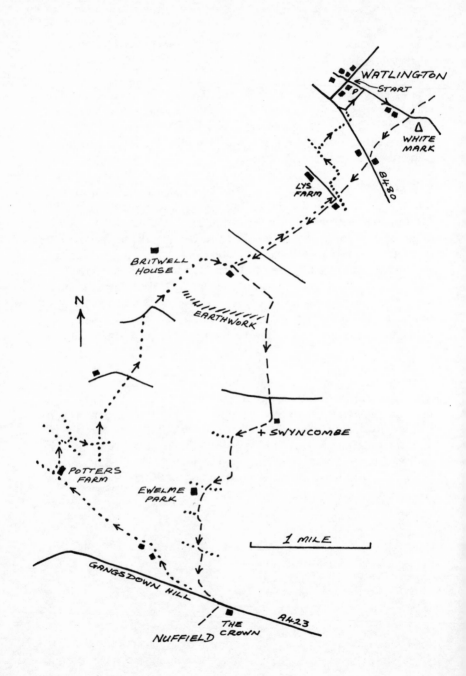

WATLINGTON

START

WHITE MARK

B480

LYS FARM

N

BRITWELL HOUSE

N

EARTHWORK

+ SWYNCOMBE

POTTERS FARM

EWELME PARK

1 MILE

GANGSDOWN HILL

A423

THE CROWN

NUFFIELD

Watlington to Nuffield

Introduction: From Watlington – or rather ½ mile south-east of Watlington – the Path follows the line of the Icknield Way as far as North Farm below Swyncombe Downs. Here it turns south towards Swyncombe itself: a secluded settlement seemingly untouched by the modern world. The Path continues in a southerly direction through Ewelme Park to the A423 road at Nuffield Common. Because there are some moderate hills to climb there are also some fine views to enjoy; of cultivated fields, of wood and downland, and of the open plain.

Distance: 5 miles (8km), including the ½ mile link from Watlington to the Ridgeway Path.

Return to Watlington: 6½ miles (10.5km), mostly along easy-going paths. No buses to speak of!

Parking in Watlington: There is an excellent free car park off Hill Road.

The Walk: The path is reached from Watlington by walking along Hill road for ½ mile to where the Path crosses the road – just beyond house No. 90. Turn right onto the Path. **(4)**After ½ mile you will reach the B480 road. On the way you have noticed Watlington Hill and Watlington Park. The house, which is visible through gaps in the trees on the left, is described by Nikolaus Pevsner as a 'neat Georgian brick box'. It was built in 1755. The Hill, which is well to the left of the house, is in the care of the National Trust and is part of a Site of Special Scientific Interest – the 'interest' being the ecology of the yew scrub.

Cross the road to the lane opposite and go along this for about ⅓ mile until it meets a five-way junction just beyond a dried-up pond. Keep straight on here (passing two large houses on your left) along a path between scrubby hedges. The path eventually comes out into the open and meets a road. Cross the road to the track opposite and go ahead (about 350 yards) until you reach a farm track going off left between a line of trees and farm buildings. Go uphill in this (you are now leaving the Icknield Way) for ⅓ mile to the lower edge of a beech wood where the track divides two ways. Take the right-hand branch which skirts the lower edge of the wood.

Looking back you will see Britwell House in its attractive setting. The house was built in 1728 for Sir Edward Simeon, and is thought to have been designed by Edward Trubshawe. Previous owners of the house were Mr David Hicks and Lady Pamela Hicks (daughter of the late Lord Mountbatten). An extensive linear earthwork, largely hidden by a line of trees and scrub, reaches out westward from the foreground along the spur of Swyncombe Down. Because of its commanding position relative to the Icknield Way it seems likely that the earthwork had a military, perhaps defensive, role. Swyncombe Down itself is another Site of Special Scientific Interest, noted for its chalk grassland flora.

Your path soon curves left and up into the wood, and then downhill to a path junction. It continues down – alongside a field – then up to meet a road. Go forward along the road to Swyncombe church; Swyncombe House is just around the corner. Now don't go dashing on: this idyllic settlement is for unhurried contemplation. Notice in particular the beautifully carved faces and wings on the headstones in the churchyard. Swyncombe House, a 'thin and half-hearted attempt at the Jacobean style', was built in about 1840.

With the church to your left, rear, and the new graveyard on your right, go through the gate ahead and along a track which gradually curves right. Ignore the first gate on the left and continue on to a stile on the left – about ¼ mile from the church. Go over this and uphill; then further uphill through the wood to emerge at the corner of a field. Go forward along the edge of the field and follow it round as it curves right to a stile and gate. A farm track will then take you

to Ewelme Park Farm; turn left here and go between the farm buildings and alongside the House itself. In 1953, on the occasion of the
planting of a tree to commemorate Queen Elizabeth II's Coronation,
a hoard of 202 Roman coins was unearthed about 300 yards south of
the house. This puts it somewhere in the 'paddock' on your left. The
hoard was subsequently placed with the Ashmolean Museum in Oxford.

After a few hundred yards the path forks beside a pond; take the
left-hand branch. After 30 yards it forks again. Take the right-hand
branch and follow this to a large field. Now you must launch yourself
across this field with your sights aimed at a white waymark post near
the right-hand end of a long narrow wood. Once in the wood go left
and, after 100 yards, right into another field; again you must aim for
a white post, this time at the near right-hand end of a square plantation. Proceed half-left uphill through the plantation to its top left-hand
corner, where a gate places you on Gangsdown Hill (A423). Turn
left for the Crown.

Returning to Watlington: With the Crown on your left go down the
A423 for ¼ mile to a lay-by on the right. It's a busy road so do please
walk on the verge! Turn half-right into a rough lane soon after this
and follow it all the way down to the second bungalow (you could
easily miss the first!). When the lane turns left just beyond the second
bungalow go forward in the path under overhanging bushes. This will
soon lead you into a field. It's more-or-less straight on now for one
mile to Potter's Farm. Spelling that out in detail: you have first a
sparse hedge on your right, followed by a solitary oak tree; then an
open barn; then the summit of the path – all the while walking parallel
to the A423 road less than ¼ mile down on your left. After the summit
you will pass between a hedge on the right and an uncultivated area
on the left before going downhill to the farm.

Turn right into the farm drive and bear left across fields after you
pass the farmhouse. You should have a fine view of Swyncombe
Down ahead. Don't go left with the drive when you reach the far
side of the fields but turn right beside an old cattle trough. After 50
yards along a grassy bridleway turn left into a narrow path running
between hedges (of a sort). The path soon meets a track – with which
it forms a T-junction. Turn right and go down to a track-crossing in

a shallow valley. Turn left here and go along for ½ mile to a road. Cross the road into a field and continue straight on, with a wire fence left. In the next field you will be accompanied by a hedge on the right – all the way to another road.

The Swan's Way sign just at the roadside refers to a 65 mile horse-riding trail. Turn right here and, when the road itself soon turns right, go straight on along a rough track with a beech wood on your right. When at the end of the wood a track comes in from the left, go forward with it; and when you see Britwell House over to your left, you will know where you are – and that you will soon be back on the Ridgeway Path.

So now you must retrace your earlier steps by going straight on for 1½ miles to the 5-way junction at the busy Lys Farm. There is a stile there – on the left – just to the right of the farm drive. Go over this and along the left-hand edge of a field to a stile in the far left-hand corner. Once over this turn right immediately and go between a hedge on the right and a farm compound (more a farm graveyard!) on the left. After 60 yards turn left at a waymark sign and cross the fields along a well-established path. Now don't go all the way to a group of trees but turn off right along the middle of a waymarked field in the direction slightly left of a distant bungalow. This will take you to the B480 Watlington road.

Go right a few paces and cross the road to an interesting stone stile opposite. Now go forward along the right-hand edge of a field to its far right-hand corner, then left between parallel hedges of elder (good stock for winemaking!). Passing a longish pond on the left and garages right, go forward to join a road. Turn right here and, near its end, left along a path to Watlington's car park.

Nuffield to Wallingford

Introduction: Now we come to the last few Chiltern miles; and what better way to descend the escarpment than to follow that magnificent green line of Grim's Dyke as it drops down from Nuffield to Mongewell Park. It is at Mongewell Park that we leave the Ridgeway Path and cross the lush river meadows to the Thames and to Wallingford.

Distance: 5 miles (8km), including the one mile link from the Ridgeway Path to Wallingford.

Return: You could return to Nuffield by bus, but why not walk back the way you came? That Grim's Dyke path is a unique experience!

Parking in Nuffield: At a lay-by on the A423, downhill from The Crown public house. Or you could drive ahead to the village, where parking is possible near the school – not far from the church; you should then ignore the next paragraph!

The Walk: Leave the A423 road at Nuffield Common along a rough drive starting from the right-hand side of The Crown public house. This takes you close to Fairway Cottage – so close that it feels like a trespass! Bear left round the cottage and follow the garden hedge to its end. You must then launch out across the golf course (keeping your head low!) and follow a line of white posts, each with an acorn waymark. Go over a stile to the right of the clubhouse, and across a field towards Nuffield Church.

Massingham's brief commentary on 'pepper-potted Nuffield

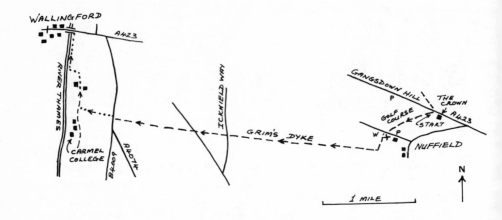

Church' was that it had 'nothing in it and was kept locked on the principle of fastening the stable door after the horse is stolen'. That was in 1940. Now you may enter freely; and there is a kind invitation from the rector to use the water tap (on the church wall) and the churchyard seat!

Back in the road and with the church on your left, go beyond a flint and brick wall to a hedge-gap leading into a field. From here, on a clear day, you will have a fine view across the Thames Valley to the Oxfordshire Plain; the scene is shared by the cooling towers at Didcot – almost mellowed by distance – and the Sinodun Hills beyond Wallingford. Follow the top left-hand edge of the field to its far left-hand corner, then go over two stiles and turn right along what you will soon realise is that enigmatic Grim's Dyke.

Now begins a descent to the Thames Valley; apart from suggesting that you cross to the right-hand side of the dyke quite soon, few directions are necessary; simply follow the line of the dyke downhill for 3 miles to the A4074 road. On your way you will cross two roads – the first is the Icknield Way – and numerous tracks. The dyke becomes indistinct at times, fading out completely at one place. On your way down you will have a pleasant bird's-eye view of Wallingford through a break in the trees. It is interesting to compare the chalkiness of the dyke, as it crosses the plateau, with the brown of the fields on either side: it seems likely that the dyke-builders extracted their materials from distant chalky sites rather than spoil adjacent fertile land. Where the thorn scrub grows thinly along this green ribbon you may notice that many species of chalk-loving wild flowers have taken hold.

The path finally reaches the A4074 road immediately opposite the entrance to Carmel College. The college – a Jewish school – hides a greater name: Mongewell Park. It was once described as 'this lovely place by the Thames' – with its late 19th-century mansion, its many forest trees, and its ornamental lake. A future prospect is that this 'lovely place' may be devastated by the proposed Wallingford by-pass.

Cross the road and go downhill for 25 yards to a path on the left. This tree-shaded path is accompanied on its left-hand side by the college drive and the continuation of Grim's Dyke. It crosses a branch of the drive and continues ahead under trees to a T-junction with a paved path.

Now comes the parting of the ways: if you are staying on the Ridgeway Path you should turn left here – and continue from **(5)** on page 55. For Wallingford turn right, and walk forward to where the paved path turns half-right. Don't turn right with it but go straight on along a tree-lined path. From the end of this path go forward along a rough drive, passing a redundant church on the left, then pass between houses on the right and barns on the left to a stile. This places you in a large meadow. Go forward 30 yards to a waymark post just beyond a cattle trough; turn left and cross to a similar post on the river bank. Turn right here and follow the Thames to Wallingford Bridge. You will need to go under the bridge in order to elevate yourself to the road.

Returning to Nuffield: Oxford Citylink coach 390/490; 2-hourly service every day.

Historical Note

Wallingford is a small but interesting Thames-side town, with a number of fine buildings, including the Corn Exchange, the Town Hall in Market Square and Lamb Arcade in High Street. I recall seeing the Arcade in a derelict condition; it has now been fully restored by a group of local people, winning an award in the process. The 'building' that is perhaps most likely to be taken for granted is the Bridge. It dates back to the 13th-century and has no less than 19 arches.

If your bus back to Nuffield is not due for an hour-or-so you could spend that time in Wallingford's modern shops (and get that weekend shopping over and done with!) or pleasantly while away the time on one of the many seats in Market Square.

Wallingford to Goring and Streatley

Introduction: Passing within a mile of Wallingford the Ridgeway Path strikes south-west from Mongewell Park along Thameside fields and meadows and through the lovely villages of North Stoke and South Stoke. From Wallingford we make our rendezvous with the Ridgeway Path by retracing the final part of the previous walk, with the Thames as welcome companion for part of the way.

Distance: 6½ miles (10.5km) including the 1 mile link from Wallingford to the Ridgeway Path at Mongewell Park.

Return: Hourly bus from Streatley.

Parking in Wallingford: There is an official car park beside the A4130 near the east bank of the Thames (the side opposite the town).

The Walk: From Wallingford go onto the Thames bridge and descend a flight of steps to the east bank (the side opposite the town). These steps are in sight of the car park mentioned above. Go under the arch here and follow the Thames bank (with the Thames on your right) along two large meadows. When nearly at the end of the second meadow (after passing Wallingford Yacht Marina on the opposite bank) a waymark post will direct you left across the meadow to a similar post on the opposite side – near a cattle trough. Turn right at this second post and pass between barns right and houses left to a rough drive. Go forward in the drive and link up with a long, narrow path after passing a church on the right. This church, being no longer in use, is maintained by the Redundant Churches Fund. The tree-lined

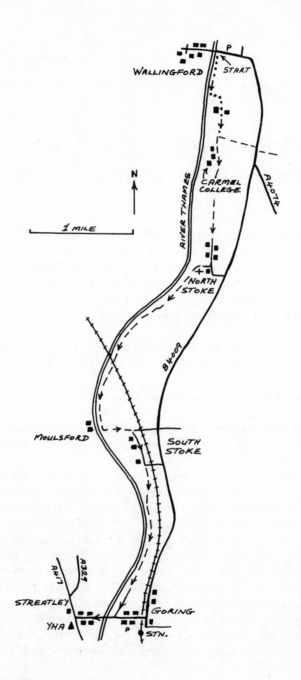

path eventually joins a paved path. You should continue forward when you see the Ridgeway Path signs.

(5)You will go alongside a pasture on the left and up to an inner entrance to Carmel College (a Jewish school). Keep straight on here, along a drive, passing houses on the right. Behind the trees on your left is the lake which was an attractive feature of the original Mongewell Park estate. At the junction in the drive go straight ahead through a gate and onto a path under tall trees. This will eventually lead you through the perimeter fence of the park. Go ahead along a path with a field left and a hedge right. The village of North Stoke is just ahead.

One of the first buildings encountered as you enter North Stoke is the beautifully restored Old Mill with the mill-stream (the Drincan) flowing beneath its walls. The Drincan runs down from a large pond behind Mill House, the pond being replenished by a spring. Following its centuries-old career in the grinding of corn and meal the Drincan was harnessed to drive a dynamo which supplied electricity to The Springs, the large house on the B4009.

Dame Clara Butt, the celebrated singer, owned two houses in the village: Brook Lodge, the pink house in view from the bridge, and Prospect House, opposite the village hall. She is remembered for her remarkable contralto voice and for her part in the first performances of a number of Sir Edward Elgar's works.

Continue through the village and turn right at the T-junction (Church Lane) just before the farmyard of Northstoke Farm. This leads to the church, where you will find much of interest – including the fine old timbers of the entrance porch and chancel roof, the medieval wall paintings and the sundial on the south-facing wall. Dame Clara Butt died in 1936 and her grave, together with that of her husband and two young sons, is close to the east end of the church. 'With her whole heart she sang songs and loved Him that made her' is a tribute to a woman who experienced sorrow along with success: one of her sons died at the age of 19, the other at 28.

Go round the right-hand side of the church through the graveyard to a stile; then forward for a short distance to follow a path with a timber fence right. After a succession of fields and stiles you are led alongside a Thameside meadow and then past the right-hand side of a house to a T-junction – where you should turn right. After a few

55

yards you will arrive at a delightful place under chestnut trees on the river bank.

Now follow the left-hand bank of the Thames for 1¼ miles across a succession of riverside meadows linked to each other by wooden gates. The path will lead you under the arches of the Moulsford railway bridge (see Historical Notes). Your 1¼ miles is up when you arrive at the busy boating centre at Moulsford. Here you must turn left into a rough track leading to South Stoke. Where the track ends at some cottages turn right into a tarred road and go ahead to a Y-junction. This is South Stoke, noted for its ancient farms, the oldest of which is Manor Farm just ahead of you. In the farmyard beyond the flint wall there is what is thought to be the second largest dovecote in the country (Yorkshire has the largest). It was built in the 16th-century and houses about 1000 pigeon nests.

Take the right-hand branch of the Y-junction and, ignoring all turnings, keep ahead through the village. At the end of the village where the road turns left to go under the railway, keep straight on along a bridleway signposted to Goring. The path runs across a field, changes to a rough drive and then to a road; houses proliferate and it becomes clear that you are in the suburbanized environs of Goring.

When the road turns left in hair-pin fashion to go over the railway keep straight on along a bridleway. After ½ mile you will meet a road coming in from the left. Go forward to its summit and join a path leaving the right-hand side opposite Clevemede housing estate. This path will take you down into Goring. On your right as you cross the bridge is Goring Lock. Together with its neighbour at Cleeve ½ mile upstream, the lock played an important part in Thames navigation when the commercial use of the river was more evident than it is today.

Returning to Wallingford: Bus route 5 from the Bull Hotel, Streatley; hourly, Mon-Sat only. Note that the last bus runs mid-afternoon Monday-Friday, early evening on Saturday.

Historical Notes

Moulsford Railway Bridge: This was built by the great 19th-century engineer Isambard Kingdom Brunel. The bridge, together with 20½ miles of the Great Western Railway from Reading to Steventon, was opened to the public on 1st June 1840. In 1893 it was doubled to its present width. The earlier span shows signs of decay, but remains in service after more than 170 years continous use.

Goring Church: Even if you are not versed in ecclesiastical matters you will agree that the unencumbered walls and the delicate tracery of the roof timbers endow this church with a beauty that is simple and refreshing. Hanging above the tower arch is an old bell which had been in use for more than 600 years – until 1929 when it was moved to its present position. To the left of the pulpit there is a memorial plaque engraved to the memory of Hugh Whistler who died on 17th January 1615 aged 216 years! While you contemplate this seemingly miraculous life-span I will sober your thoughts with the popular notion that the engraver was a little careless in his art!

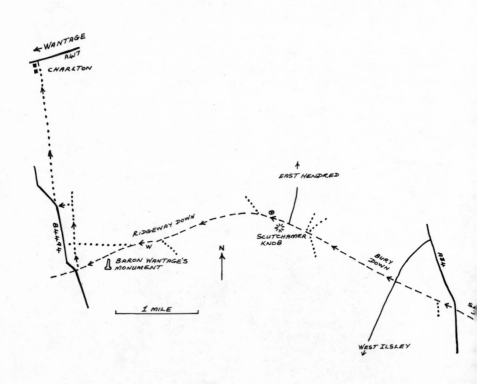

Goring and Streatley to Wantage

Introduction: From Streatley the Path follows the near straight line of the ancient Ridgeway westward along the Oxfordshire Downs. Included in the breathtaking views along this first part of the downs is the distant Chiltern escarpment – a reminder of more pastoral aspects of the Ridgeway Path. If you enjoy a long invigorating walk, one that tests your stamina and gives you a sense of achievement at the end of the day, then this is for you! But do carry plenty of sustenance: there is a water tap at the half-way point on Several Down, but no shops or cafes anywhere along the route!

Distance: 15½ miles (24.9km). If this is too much like a marathon, you could leave the Ridgeway Path at Compton Downs and divert to East Ilsley, making a total of 7 miles. Returning from East Ilsley is difficult, if not impossible – except by taxis!

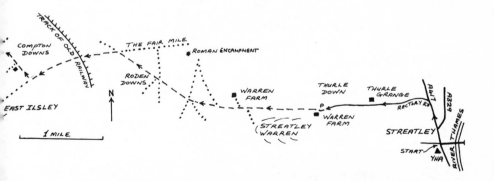

Return from Wantage: Bus to Didcot, then train to Goring.

Parking in Goring: Simply follow the public car park signs from the main street near the church; or you may find a slot in Manor Road.

In Streatley it's more difficult, unless you drive the first part of the Ridgeway Path and drop anchor in Rectory Road.

The Walk: From the main crossroads at the centre of Streatley go along the A329 road in the direction of Moulsford and Wallingford (a right turn if you have just crossed the Thames from Goring). After ¼ mile the main road divides into the A417 and the A329. Take the left-hand branch – the A417 – and go along this for ⅓ mile to Rectory Road on the left. The entrance to Rectory Road is marked by a letter-box and a 'No Through Road' sign.

Go along Rectory Road for 1½ miles to Warren Farm. From the farm entrance (there is a post box here) you should bear right and go uphill along a wide track. This climbs steadily for quite some distance and is accompanied by the impressive expanse of Streatley Warren. Ancient cultivation terraces can be seen at the head of the Warren; these are thought to date back to Iron Age times. There is another Warren Farm at the top. Don't go down the farm drive but keep straight on. Avoid paths going off to the right as you descend to a somewhat complicated junction ½ mile from the summit. Take the left fork here; this passes a group of hawthorn trees on the right and then an incoming track on the left.

If you have time to spare you could turn off right at the fork and walk ½ mile to the site of the 4th-century Roman encampment on Lowbury Hill. A great quantity of Roman pots, as well as bricks, tiles, coins and oyster shells has been found in and around the encampment. Apparently, a female skeleton with its skull smashed in was found buried in the foundations of a stone wall!

If this grim detail has set you against the diversion, you should continue on for ½ mile to another track junction. Keeping straight on here, you will pass a wood on your right almost immediately. After yet another ½ mile the track cuts deeply into the chalk – just before a Y-junction. Fork left here along a double track. The Ridgeway Path has taken leave of the true Ridgeway for the time being and follows instead the Roman Fair Mile across Compton Downs.

The way ahead crosses a bridge over a disused railway. This is a relic of the Didcot, Newbury and Southampton Joint Railway (see Historical Notes). Looking back over your right shoulder as you climb the next uphill track you should see two Bronze Age burial mounds (bell barrows). These are about ¾ mile away, in line with tree-capped Churn Hill. Excavation has revealed a cremation burial and a Bronze Age dagger at one of these.

Once over the hill you will meet a concrete crossing drive. If East Ilsley is your destination you should cross the drive and go ahead for ¾ mile to a road. Turn right there for East Ilsley. Otherwise, turn right and go past the entrance to an Agricultural Research Council property. The concrete drive gives way to a grassy track. The track soon curves left and then right before running alongside a horse gallop over Several Down. On a clear day you will see the distant escarpment of the Chiltern Hills, punctuated by the monument on Coombe Hill, Wendover, and the plume of smoke from the Chinnor cement works. The near view is of course dominated by the Didcot cooling towers,

Where two paths join the Ridgeway on the left you will find a water tap – put there especially for Ridgeway walkers (there are some very kind, thoughtful people at Oxfordshire County Council!). An underpass will take you safely to the far side of the A34 and back on to the Ridgeway. Go along this for almost a mile to a by-road (this leads to the pretty village of West Ilsley, 1 mile south). The two tall chimneys down there on the plain identify for you the Atomic Energy Research Establishment. Cross the by-road and continue ahead for 1¼ miles to the point where a road (from East Hendred) terminates. Situated in the wood on the left there is what was once a very large mound called Schutchamer Knob (see Historical Notes).

Continuing ahead along the Ridgeway you will soon pass an Ordnance Survey plinth on your right. Two miles further on the path divides two ways. Take the left uphill branch leading to Lord Wantage's Monument (see Historical Notes). This is a good place for a breather and a sit-down!

In about ½ mile you will arrive at the B4494 Wantage Road. Turn to (6) on page 68 if you are continuing on the Path. To terminate your day in Wantage you should go through a gate about 50 yards before the junction of the Ridgeway Path with the road; this leads into a steeply sloping field at the lowest (right-hand) corner of which is another gate. Go through this and onto a path which runs alongside a horse gallop. Turn left 100 yards after passing a small plantation. This takes you back to the B4494. Turn right and follow the long, straight, tiresome track (not the B4494) to Charlton on the A417. Turn left here for Wantage.

Returning to Goring: 302 bus from Wantage Market Square to Didcot Station (an interesting ride through the villages of Lockinge, East Hendred and Harwell); hourly service Mon-Sat only. The last bus goes late afternoon! The train from Didcot to Goring runs hourly every day.

Historical Notes

The Didcot, Newbury and Southampton Joint Railway: The Didcot-Newbury section of this railway (the Berkshire Downs part) was opened in 1882. The promoters' dream of a trunk route carrying a heavy volume of traffic to and from Southampton was not realised, due largely to the lack of interest on the part of the operating company, the G.W.R. It was a commercial failure and a disaster for the shareholders. But the line did have one moment of glory, for it is said that during the 12 months prior to D-Day (6th June 1944) about 16,000 military trains rode the metals to Southampton.

Scutchamer Knob: This mound, which is mentioned in the Saxon Chronicles of AD 1006, was severely mutilated by 19th-century archaeologists; its height was originally 77 feet, but it is now little more than a shell with walls a few feet high. Included among the insignificant 'finds' were fragments of Iron Age pottery, an iron buckle and a large charred oak post, but no internment.

Lord Wantage's Monument: This was erected in memory of Colonel Sir Robert James Loyd-Linsey, Baron Wantage of Lockinge, V.C., K.C.B., who died in 1901. For those who are none the wiser, I quote from *Wantage, Past and Present* (by A. Gibbons and E.C. Davey, 1901): 'It is impossible within the limits of this notice to give any adequate idea of the fullness of Lord Wantage's life, or the great extent of the useful, patriotic and philanthropic labours in which he was engaged up to almost the moment of his death'. He was a 'driving force' in the early days of the Didcot, Newbury and Southampton Joint Railway, a distinguished soldier of the Crimean War, and one of the first recipients of the Victoria Cross. His prominent position on the Downs is well earned!

Wantage: Not a spectacular town in terms of individual buildings but the total effect is pleasant and homely. Here, as elsewhere, such simple qualities are not enough to prevent the encroachment of the developer; so enjoy it while you may. Alfred the Great's statue stands at one end of the square. He was born in Wantage in AD849. To the south of the square, in Portway, the Wantage Museum holds an interesting collection of exhibits relating to the history and archaeology of the Vale of the White Horse and the town itself.

Wantage is of particular interest to the tram enthusiast. It was the first town in England to operate a steam-powered tram service. This was inaugurated in 1876 and ran from the town to Wantage Road Station on the G.W.R., a distance of 2½ miles. Passenger services ceased in 1925, freight in 1945.

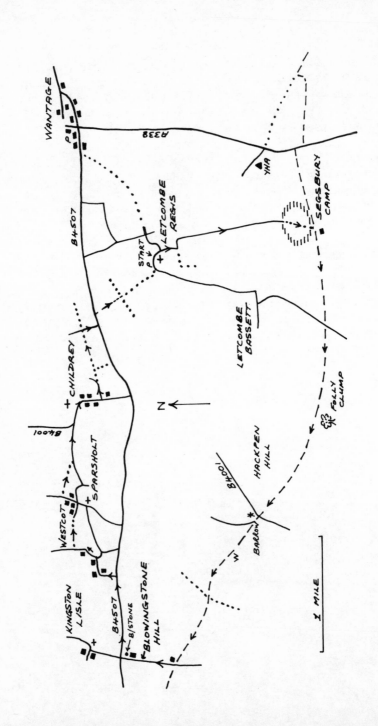

Wantage to Blowingstone Hill

Introduction: This is an opportunity to enjoy another invigorating and unhindered walk along the downs, to marvel at the splendour of Hackpen Hill, and to exercise our lungs on the Blowingstone! And for the return journey we have a preview – in Sparsholt and in Childrey – of the delightful villages of the Vale of the White Horse.

Although my directions commence at Wantage it makes good sense to ignore the first paragraph and start from Letcombe Regis Church. The round trip ends there and the mileage is reduced.

For those who have twigged that nearly 2 miles of the Ridgeway Path have been left out of the intinerary (from the B4494 to Segsbury Camp) and who insist on covering every inch, there is no choice but to walk the final part (that long dusty track) of the previous walk in reverse. Directions for this can be found at the end of this chapter.

Distance: 6 miles (9.7km), including two links with the Ridgeway Path totalling 2 miles – one from Letcombe Regis, the other at Blowingstone Hill.

Return: 4 miles (6.4km) along easy-going paths and roads back to Letcombe Regis. Add a total of 2½ miles (4km) if starting from Wantage.

Parking: At Letcombe Regis it is just about possible to park near to the school or the church. Wantage has a large car park beside the museum; and there are free roadside slots in Ormond Road near the fire station.

65

The Walk: A narrow metalled path leaves the B4507 (Portway) oppo-site Priory Road in Wantage, just a short distance beyond the new Recreation Centre. The Civic Hall car park and King Alfred's School are close by. You simply follow this path all the way to Letcombe Regis – alongside Letcombe Brook and into a road running through the centre of a small housing estate. Go straight over the crossroads at the other end of the estate (there is a telephone box here) and follow the road round to the church. According to one commentator the church was 'severely manhandled' in 1863. You may wish to break off at this point and make up your own mind on the matter!

From Letcombe Regis church cross over to the road signposted 'Village and Downs only' and continue through the village to a left-hand turn. There is a signpost here 'Ridgeway 1¼ miles'. Don't go down there for you will miss Segsbury Camp and even more of the Ridgeway, but follow the road first left and then right and uphill to the Camp on Castle Hill. Although Iron Age in origin, Segsbury Camp – now just a large circular rampart – was modified in Saxon times. In 1871 fragments of human bones, pieces of pottery and flint scrapers were found here in a flint cist beneath a sarsen stone. The route through the centre of the camp leads directly to the Ridgeway, where you should turn right.

(7)The Ridgeway now climbs gently to the summit of Rats Hill. At ½ mile intervals you will meet first a track, then a road, both leading down to Letcombe Bassett in the lee of the downs (for your interest only!). A few yards beyond the road we have a dramatic transition from the hedged track which has been a familiar feature of the Ridge-way so far; and with massive Hackpen Hill in pride of place. A summit of the path is reached soon after passing the weather-worn copse of beech trees called Folly Clump. If your eyesight is keen you will just make out a small burial mound on Hackpen Hill above the head of a combe called Devil's Punchbowl. You should also have a good view of Letcombe Regis – with Wantage beyond.

In less than 1 mile you will arrive at the B4001 road. Cross this to the metalled road opposite. The mound in a field immediately to your right is a bowl barrow. This was excavated by Greenwell in the 19th-century and an 'unaccompanied primary cremation' found. About 100 yards beyond the B4001 you must leave the metalled road by turning half-left into a dusty track. After ½ mile the path curves left and slopes downhill to a crossing track. Before descending you may care to identify the villages of Kingston Lisle, Sparsholt and Childrey at the foot of the Downs. Directly ahead of you at a distance of 2 miles is 856ft Whitehorse Hill.

After the crossing track the Ridgeway goes over a hill to meet the Kingston Lisle road above Blowingstone Hill. There is a large green corrugated-iron barn just here. Turn right and go down the hill – unless you are continuing on the Ridgeway, in which case turn to **(8)** on page 71. The piece of sarsen stone known as the Blowingstone and immortalized in *Tom Brown's Schooldays* stands beside a cottage garden at the bottom of the hill. It has a hole through which can be blown a low-pitched wailing note – or so it is said! Legend has it that the stone was used by King Alfred as a trumpet to call his soldiers together. Go on – have a blow!

Returning to Letcombe Regis: From Blowingstone Hill turn right into the B4507, signposted to Wantage and Childrey. Take the first road on the left for Westcot and go right with this through the village. Turn left at the T-junction at the end of the road (there is a very welcome seat just here!) and go downhill in Westcot Lane for less than ¼ mile to the last house on the right 'Field View'. A footpath signpost just before the house (you should have ignored an earlier signpost on the right) directs you across a large field, with a hedge on the right initially. You must aim for the nearest brick-built house on the far side of the field. If the going is rough (the path ploughed up) take heart: you are doing valiant service for the footpath lobby!

From that house go along a road (West Street) to a T-junction opposite a public house. This is Sparsholt. Turn left into Watery Lane and go along this for 85 yards to a large white house on the left (timber-framed on its far side) then through a gap in the hedge on the roadside opposite the house. With an old orchard on your right cross the field to an equally old iron kissing-gate under a hawthorn tree (left of a hedge-gap), then straight on to a hedge-gap after crossing a large field. You will have passed a stand of tall trees on your right. From this last hedge-gap you should go ½-right across a field to a waymark post at a road – to the left of a house. Turn left in the road and follow it to the B4001 road – at a 'give way' sign – and go forward to Childrey.

Turn right into Childrey High Street – passing the village pond on your left. Once you have escaped the attentions of the village geese turn first or second left into 'Stowhill'. When this bears left go forward along a tarmac bridleway (at a 'no through road' sign). Stay on this path all the way to its summit – where it meets a road. Turn right here and go uphill to the busy B4507, in which turn left. Only 100 yards of this before you see a waymarked path on the right – just where the road begins to climb. This good path will take you over a crossing and down into Letcombe Regis. When you reach the Letcombe Bassett road at a bend you will find the church (and your car – I hope!) directly ahead.

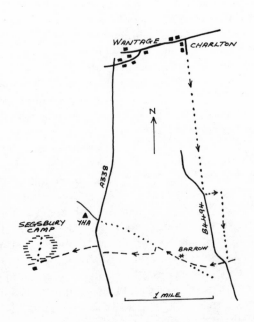

Map showing alternative route from Wantage to The Ridgeway Path.

Wantage to the Ridgeway – Alternative Route: At the eastern end of Wantage at Charlton, Lark Hill starts from the A417 road just beyond the Lord Nelson public house. From the top of Lark Hill a long straight track runs south for 1½ miles. Where this meets the B4494 road you should turn left into a path. Go along this for ¼ mile and turn right at a T-junction in the path; you will pass a small wood on your right and a horse gallop on your left. Ahead a gate leads into a steeply sloping field; in the top right-hand corner of the field another gate leads on to the Ridgeway. (**6**)Cross the B4494 Wantage road to the track opposite. After 200 yards the track turns left; don't turn left with it but go straight on. About ½ mile further on (where you are met by another track coming in from the left, rear) there is a grass-covered tumulus immediately to the right of the path. A bronze awl and a bronze riveted dagger were found here when the tumulus was excavated in 1938.

After another ½ mile you must turn left into what soon becomes a metalled farm track (unless you are staying at Court Hill Youth Hostel: in which case continue straight on). If in doubt about your position, there should be a cottage behind trees on the right (north). The farm track takes you past Whitehouse Farm and to the A338 road. Turn right in the A338 and in about 200 yards – just before a house on the left – turn left along a stony track. After ½ mile you will see the rampart of Segsbury Camp. You can get a closer look and enjoy a stroll along the rampart by turning right at a farm crossing ahead. Continue from (**7**) on page 66.

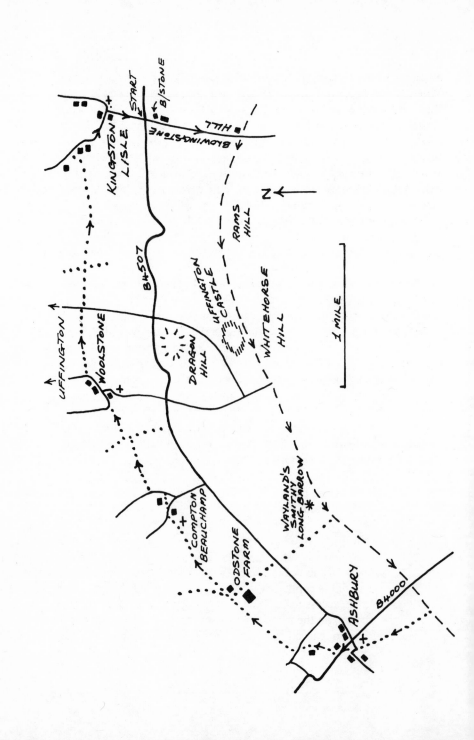

Blowingstone Hill to Ashbury

Introduction: Iron Age Uffington 'Castle', the White Horse of Uffington, and the Wayland's Smithy Long Barrow are the undisputed highlights of this stretch of the Ridgeway – perhaps of the entire Ridgeway. And as if that wasn't enough, our return walk is along footpaths linking four of the lovely settlements that lie at the foot of the Downs: Ashbury, Compton Beauchamp, Woolstone and Kingston Lisle.

Distance: 5 miles (8km), including two ½ mile links with the Ridgeway Path – at Ashbury and at Blowingstone Hill.

Return: 5 miles (8km) easy and level walking.

Parking: There is space for one or two cars at the bottom of Blowingstone Hill where it meets the B4507 south of Kingston Lisle. You could park at the top of the hill where it meets the Ridgeway, but first remove all valuables from your car!

The Walk: From the B4507 go up Blowingstone Hill for ½ mile to a large green barn on the left. Turn right here on to the Ridgeway. (8)The first landmark is Whitehorse Hill 1½ miles from the Kingston Lisle road. The hill is capped by the extensive ramparts of Iron Age Uffington Castle, access to which is through a gate on the right. Over the brow of the hill on the north-facing slope is the magnificent White Horse of Uffington, carved out of the turf (see Historical Notes). On the downland side of the Icknield Way is the flat-topped Dragon Hill where St. George is reputed to have killed the Dragon. The bare

71

patch is where its blood poured out!

Back on the Ridgeway you will soon pass a gap in the fence on your right. (This – for your information only – is the way to the car park and ice-cream van!) 1¼ miles further on and just off the Ridgeway, is Wayland's Smithy Long Barrow, under a magnificent stand of beech trees (see Historical Notes). After another ¾ mile you will arrive at the B4000 Lambourn-Ashbury road. If you now look in a southerly direction (left with respect to the Ridgeway ahead) in line with the right-hand edge of a large wood you will see (binoculars assumed) the green mound of Alfred's Castle about 1½ miles away. This small Iron Age camp was robbed of much of its stone work during the building of Ashdown Park, a country house nearby.

Now I hope you can judge one quarter of a mile, because that's the precise distance from the B4000 to the footpath turn-off for Ashbury. (If you are continuing on the Ridgeway turn to (9) on page 75). Look for a gap in the hedge on the right opposite a waymark post inscribed with 'C.R.' (an Oxfordshire County Council 'Circular Route'). On my last visit the hedge-gap had an iron gate permanently held open. Go through the gap and proceed along the border between two fields – at right angles to the Ridgeway. This will take you down into Ashbury.

Returning to Blowingstone Hill: From the war memorial in Ashbury go past the Rose & Crown and turn first left into the B4000; then turn right along a tarmac path beside the Evangelical Church. This will take you to a lake and in an uphill left-hand curve to a road. Go left a few paces and cross the road to a footpath and two iron gates. Turn right after the second gate and go over a farm crossing to a wide, level path under electricity poles. You will eventually cross a stile, then another very soon, before entering a field at its bottom right-hand corner. Go briefly uphill in this field and aim for the stile about half-way along its far edge. Someone has kindly marked out the route from here onwards with splashes of white paint, and these will guide you all the way to Compton Beauchamp.

Cross the next field to another stile, then along a track that passes 50 yards to the left of a white-walled cottage terrace. (Odstone Farm is further up on the right.) Straight on now – over stiles and along the upper edge of sloping fields, eventually to cross a horticultural plot towards a white waymark disc. Go through a kissing-gate just here and down towards Compton Beauchamp Church (Beauchamp: beautiful field; and indeed it is!).

A gate adjacent to the churchyard will place you on the church path – in which you should turn left. This will soon take you down to a road, from where you have a view of the Manor House – over your right shoulder. Follow the road as it curves right and uphill and go through a gate on the left about half-way up. Continue uphill, but now across a meadow to a stile at the left side of a group of farm buildings. A short path will soon place you in a lane in front of a bungalow (with thatched cottages nearby). Turn right in the lane and join a road at a T-junction – where you should turn left.

Proceed down the road to a stile on the right beside a 'Knighton' road sign, then very soon to a stile at a ditch (fields now in view on the left). A few paces will then place you on a path under hedges and between fields. After another stile the edge of a large field ahead will lead you to a waymark sign in its far left-hand corner. Turn left (under trees) soon after this, and right to a stile after 50 yards. Then go along the right-hand edge of two fields towards a farm building and houses – with a fine view of Uffington White Horse and Castle on the Downs to your right. A stile near the farm building will lead you out to the road at Woolstone. The White Horse pub is straight on. Continue forward from the road junction – in the direction of Uffington and Farringdon. (And what a lovely place Woolstone is: it makes all this tramping worthwhile!)

When the road turns left (ignore all lesser meanderings) go over a stile on the right leading into a field. You will see Uffington Church in the distance half-left (*Tom Brown's Schooldays* and all that!). Now you have a succession of field edges and stiles to take you straight and level for ½ mile to a road. A right turn in the road will give you a good view of Dragon Hill and 25 yards of the road will place you beside a gate on the left. The gate will send you on your way along the right-hand edge of a large field to a stile in its far right-hand corner.

You may need to search for the path across the next – very large – field. When found, aim for a gate midway along the far edge of the field (you may not see the gate from this distance). Your next aim is slightly right of a farm complex ahead, which should take you through a hedge-gap. Go slightly right again in the direction of tall trees to a stile of sorts (more a low fence) in another hedge-gap; then half-left to another stile and half-left again to an iron gate between thatched cottages. Turn right in the road ahead and follow this uphill to the junction at Kingston Lisle. Turn right for Blowingstone Hill.

Historical Notes

The White Horse of Uffington: The age and original purpose of this chalk monument are controversial, but it seems likely that it was first cut by Iron Age man, in view of its similarity to the figures that appear on coins of that period and the close proximity of an Iron Age fort. The cleaning of the Horse (the 'scouring') was an important part of the open-air festivals that took place on the hill at intervals of seven years or so until 1857. These were great occasions for games, competitions, dancing, singing and drinking. It was reported that 30,000 people attended the festival in the year 1780. A local saying tells us that 'while men sleep, the Horse climbs up the Hill'. This is not as outrageous as it sounds, for as the soil falls away from the upper edges and exposes more of the chalk, and the lower edges silt up and become colonized by grass, so the horse does indeed climb the hill!

Wayland's Smithy Long Barrow: The site was excavated 1962-3 and was found to consist of one burial chamber overlaid by another. Both have been dated at about the middle of the Neolithic period (New Stone Age). The excellent state of 'preservation' of the barrow is largely due to its reconstruction in 1964. The legend of Wayland the Smith was that he 'made swords none could resist and winged armour that carried one over the land like an eagle'. And he would shoe a traveller's horse if a penny was left on one of the stones!

Ashbury to Wanborough

Introduction: This will be another day of contrasts: the high open downs with the attendant opportunity to 'step-it-out' unhindered by any vicissitudes in the Path, and the lowland return through attractive villages and along lesser-known paths. Of the five villages along the homeward journey Bishopstone is the jewel, with its mill pond and its thatched and whitewashed cottages 'enchantingly hidden and devious among gardens'.

Distance: 5½ miles (8.9km), including two links with the Ridgeway Path totalling 2 miles.

Return: 4 miles (6.4km) walking or by bus.

Parking in Ashbury: There is a wide verge on the B4000 road uphill from Ashbury.

The Walk: From the right-hand side of the Rose & Crown go uphill along the church drive; then along a tarmac path to the right of the church. When the path turns right – to a graveyard – continue uphill in a field path. This soon curves left to meet an upcoming track. Turn right here and go uphill along the border between two fields. This will take you up to the Ridgeway – a wide track – where you should turn right.

(9)After ½ mile the Ridgeway crosses a farm track (for Idstone), where there is a water tap thoughtfully and kindly placed (a tea-urn would be more to my liking!). ⅓ mile beyond the next road-crossing a signpost at a gate points down a gulley to 'Bishopstone'. This makes

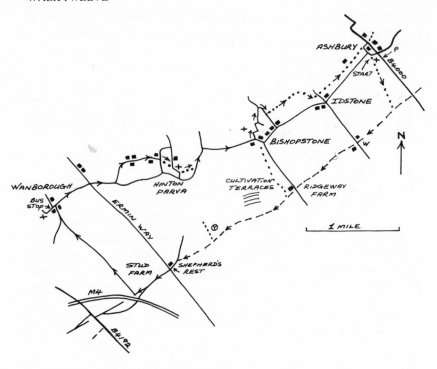

a fine walk (not today perhaps!) and offers a good view of the impressive cultivated terraces above Bishopstone (see Historical Notes).

As you proceed uphill from this point you should see – over your left shoulder – Ashdown House about 2 miles eastward. The house was built in 1665 for Queen Elizabeth of Bohemia, sister of Charles I, by her admirer the first Lord Craven. 'A perfect doll's house' is Nikolaus Pevsner's apt description of this neat four-storeyed house with cupola and golden ball. Part of the house was placed in the care of the National Trust in 1956.

After ½ mile or so you will cross the south-eastern flank of Charlbury Hill, on the top of which is an Ordnance Survey plinth. Another ½ mile further on the Ridgeway forms a T-junction with a road. Turn left in this and go forward to a crossroad by The Shepherd's Rest – the only pub on the Ridgeway and a halting place of shepherds and drovers in times past (and the only pub with such an outrageous road sign alongside!). Cross to the road opposite and continue straight ahead, with the grounds of a stud farm (King Edward's Place) on your right.

Leave the Ridgeway Path by turning right into a side road just before the M4 crossing. (If you are staying in the Ridgeway Path you should cross the M4 and turn left into the B4192; then continue from **(10)** on page 81.) The side road itself turns right when just short of the M4, and makes a long straight beeline for Wanborough. In view on the left is Liddington Hill, the undulations on its summit identifying the Iron Age fort. When you meet a road coming in from the left continue straight on into Wanborough.

Returning to Ashbury: Bus 47; 2-hourly Mon-Sat only.

Walking Back: With Wanborough's Calley Arms on your left, turn right out of Ham Road and walk along the country road for ½ mile to a crossroads. Go straight on here and take the next left turn – for Hinton Parva. After ½ mile the road through the village turns sharp right just beyond Chestnut Cottage – at a T-junction of sorts (you must ignore earlier bends in the road). Go forward from this point along a tarmac path across fields to a chapel; then follow a roadside path to Hinton Parva Church.

Turn left immediately after the church; and when the road soon turns right, go straight on along a path to a kissing-gate, passing a graveyard on the left. Cross a meadow to another gate – beside a cattle trough – then slightly left across a field to an awkward stile at a road. (If mud is a problem you could retreat to the village and arrive at the same point by making three successive left turns.) Go left in the road and downhill to a junction; then turn right for Bishopstone. A good path under lime trees will take you the last 100 yards or so into the village.

Now whatever else you do, don't fail to explore the inner sanctums of this lovely village! The best way to do this is by the path running alongside the school – opposite the phone box. Having done this you should turn left in the road just beyond the phone box (with your back to the school) and, after passing the Royal Oak, follow the twists and turns of the road until it joins another road. Turn left here and hairpin right quite soon at a junction. After about 150 yards leave the road for a wide track on the left, signposted to Idstone. This will eventually lead you into a field and to a pair of gates in its far right-hand corner. Walk half-right across a meadow and join a field-edge which is also going that way. Go left with the field-edge after a few hundred yards and aim for the 'right-most' of 3 farm gates – the one beside a pond. A stile here will lead you to a farm drive (Lower Idstone Farm) and on to the 'rough end' of a road at Idstone.

Cross to an iron gate opposite and straight on (and level) across a field to a pair of stiles at a ditch, passing a hedge and gardens on the right initially. Go forward along the right-hand edge of a field to a stile at a farm crossing; then forward again to a stile in the far left-hand corner of a field. A grassy bank will then take you past an isolated cottage on the left and to a stile in the far left-hand corner of a field. Ignore a stile on the left soon after this and go ahead to the road at Ashbury. Turn first right for the Rose & Crown – unless the seat beside the war memorial will suffice!

Historical Notes

Bishopstone: Alfred Williams in his book *Villages of the White Horse* (published in 1913), gives an interesting account of day-to-day life in Bishopstone. Of two of the village industries he wrote 'almost every day the huge wheel of the mill revolves under the weight of the foaming water, and rumbles beneath the high wall. The school, the blacksmith's shop, and the mill are all close together, the children are happy in their situation, and in the opportunities they have for viewing the several industries; they throng around the smithy door, and peer over at the mighty wheel each time they pass along, delighted to see the gleaming waters leaping down, and to view the merry fizzing sparks shooting out underneath the stroke of the blacksmith's hammer.'

The parish church is a fine building in an attractive setting. Inside there is an interesting font, fragments of medieval coloured glass, and a thought-provoking epitaph – a sermon in stone to Charles Curtis who escaped shipwreck in 1822. In Alfred Williams' day a curfew bell was rung every night from eight until nine during the foggy months as a guide for those who might be lost on the Downs.

The Cultivation Terraces: These are on the hillside above Bishopstone and can be seen from a footpath that runs from Bishopstone to the Downs. At close range they are very impressive indeed: giant-size steps cut into the hillside. While the purpose of these terraces is quite clear – that of growing crops on level ground under the protection of the hillside – their age can only be guessed at. The Bronze Age seems the most likely. The site was ideally situated below the ridge-top but well above the uninhabitable vale: a compromise that would have become increasingly inessential as time progressed.

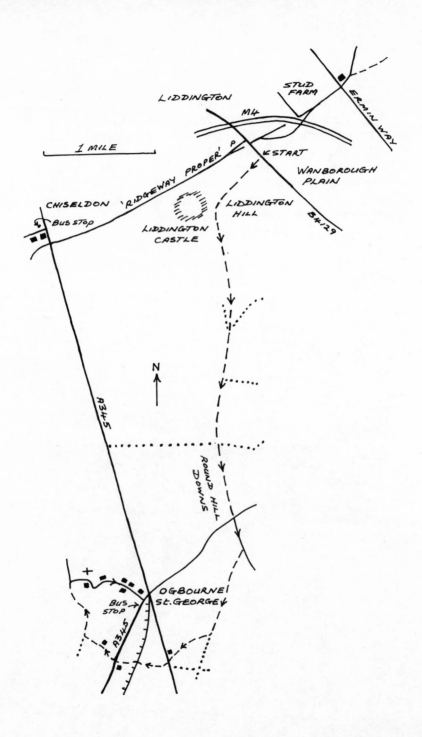

Wanborough Plain to Ogbourne St. George

Introduction: The Ridgeway Path now takes leave of the Ridgeway proper (which strikes its own low-level course direct to Hackpen Hill on the Marlborough Downs) and climbs away from the noisy M4 motorway into the quiet air on Liddington Hill. We can then take stock of another plain: that impressive U-shaped expanse overlooked by Liddington Hill and Burderop Down. After following upland by-ways we conclude with a circuitous approach to Ogbourne St. George, gleaning all the attractions of that ancient village.

Distance: 7 miles (11.3km), including a ½ mile link from the Ridgeway Path to Ogbourne.

Return: Bus to Chiseldon followed by a 1½ mile (2.4km) road walk back to Wanborough Plain.

Parking at Wanborough Plain: On the Ridgeway proper (see above) where it meets the B4192 (previously the A419) one mile south-east of Liddington (grid ref. 216805). You could tuck your car away in a short abandoned side road just here – if you wish.

The Walk: As you come out of the 'Ridgeway proper' turn right into the B4192. **(10)**Go along this – in the direction of Aldbourne – for 200 yards to an uphill track on the right. This will take you up to Liddington Hill. The small clump of beech trees ahead does not mark the summit of the Hill; this is ½ mile further on. There is, however, a good view from the far side of the clump. The track levels out and appears to be heading for the ramparts of Iron Age Liddington Castle on top of the Hill, but curves away to the left without making contact. It is unfortunate that no right of way exists between the Ridgeway and the Castle.

The Ordnance Survey plinth on the ramparts of the castle has a plaque engraved in honour of Richard Jefferies and Alfred Williams. Alfred Williams' book *Villages of the White Horse* makes good reading for Ridgeway walkers. Jefferies' birthplace Coate Farm, near Coate Water Country Park, is some 3 miles away on this side of Swindon and houses a small museum (open Wed, Sat and Sun, 2-5 p.m.).

After the Path passes its point of nearest approach to the castle it curves left to a gate and follows a hawthorn hedge before breaking out into open country. Barbury Castle, that other Iron Age hill-fort through which we will pass on tomorrow's walk, is now at a distance of 5 miles to the south-west (half-right if you are facing the Path ahead). The Path now follows the edges of two large fields in succession. It then goes right for 20 yards at a 'byway' junction and forward again into a hedge-lined track.

At this point it is worth noting that I have concluded today's walk at the far side of Ogbourne St. George in order to reduce tomorrow's mileage; so don't lose heart if you seem to be forever heading in the wrong direction. There are numerous short-cuts down to Ogbourne hereafter and you need not stay the course to the bitter end.

After emerging from the hedge-lined track you will be following the border between two large fields to the Aldbourne – Ogbourne road. Cross to the road opposite, signposted 'Chasewoods Farm'. Go along this for ¼ mile to the start of a wood (on the left) just before the road curves left, and turn off half-right along a rough track. You now have ¾ mile of path running almost straight and level to a crossing track beside an overgrown brick-built structure (all that's left of a wind pump, I believe). Turn right at the crossing and follow the track as it curves left and runs downhill to a road beside a new house. Cross to the path opposite and follow this down to the A345 road by some thatched cottages. You will pass 'under' a decapitated railway bridge on the way down. This line was once an important north-south link between the Great Western Railway at Swindon and the London and South-Western Railway at Andover. The Swindon-Marlborough section was opened in 1881.

Cross over the A345 to a 'No Through Road' signposted to Hallam.

This road meanders through an attractive cottage settlement and, after crossing the river Og, evolves into a stony track. Turn right at the T-junction ahead and go along a very pleasant path to a road. If you are continuing on the Ridgeway Path turn to (11) on page 84. For Ogbourne turn right in the road.

Returning to Wanborough Plain: Bus 70 to Chiseldon; hourly Mon-Sat only.

Alight from the bus at the junction of New Road with the A345, turn right, then first left after 150 yards into a long, straight road. This is the 'Ridgeway proper' and after 1½ miles, will take you back to your car.

Historical Note

Liddington Hill: The hill is often referred to as Richard Jefferies' 'Mount of Meditation' on account of the many excursions this 19th-century essayist is reputed to have made to the hill. The following extract from his little book *The Story of my Heart* adequately portrays his feelings. 'There was a hill to which I used to resort at such periods. The labour of walking three miles to it, all the while ascending, seemed to clear my blood of the heaviness accumulated at home. On a warm summer day the slow continued rise required continual effort, which carried away the sense of oppression. The familiar everyday scene was soon out of sight. I came to other trees, meadows and fields; I began to breathe a new air and to have a fresher aspiration . . . moving up to the sweet, short turf, at every step my heart seemed to obtain a wider horizon of feeling; with every inhalation of the rich, pure air, a deeper desire. The very light of the sun was whiter and more brilliant here.'

Ogbourne St. George
to Overton Hill

Introduction: This final invigorating walk along the Ridgeway Path crosses the magnificent open landscape of the Marlborough Downs; a landscape typical of Wiltshire but unlike anything we have seen so far. Smeathe's Ridge, Barbury Castle, Hackpen Hill, Avebury Down – each an experience to remember!

Distance: 9½ miles (15.3km).

Return: Infrequent bus to Marlborough then hourly bus to Ogbourne.

Parking at Ogbourne: It is possible to park in the wide road not far from the Post Office.

The Walk: From the T-junction near the post office go past the New Inn and all the way through the village to its far end, where a large chestnut tree stands on the lawn of March House. Turn left with the road here and right at the next bend. You are now on the Ridgeway Path. (11)Go forward in the road for about 100 yards, then left into a concrete drive. The drive soon becomes a track and divides three ways at a stile and gate. Take the middle way – the one going straight on. The Path runs along the hillside, and up to Smeathe's Ridge, overlooking a deep coombe on the left. Now you should correctly keep to the path close to the summit of the ridge, but if the day is good a short diversion to the edge of the coombe is well worthwhile for the sake of the view.

The ridge leads on to a mile-long path ending at a T-junction at Upper Herdswick, where there is a signpost giving directions to Barbury Castle and Marlborough. Turn right here and go past a bungalow and a farm. You should normally turn off left opposite the farm along a path to Iron Age Barbury Castle, but by continuing along what is now a made-up road to a field on the right you will have the opportunity to see a sarsen stone inscribed in honour of Richard Jefferies and Alfred Williams. An extensive area of primitive cultivation fields, probably dating from Iron Age or Roman times, is laid downfield below the sarsen stone. They survive as little more than rectangular markings on the ground best seen from the road below.

By now you will have realized that Barbury Castle has been taken in hand, with toilets, a car park, and an information kiosk provided. You could be forgiven for thinking that the car park and Barbury Castle are one and the same thing. The Castle is in fact further on and is approached from a gate in the far left-hand corner of the car park.

If you climb the north-facing rampart of the castle you will see a small wooded enclosure, marked on the map as 'Beranburgh 556', about ½ mile in the direction of Swindon. This is the site of a crucial battle that took place about AD 556 between the invading Saxons and the Romano-British inhabitants. Let Alfred Williams paint the scene: 'Here the Britons, burning to avenge their defeat of a few years earlier, assembled a mighty host of their bravest warriors to oppose the Saxons. But neither choice of ground, nor the tradition of Roman tactics, nor heroic Celtic valour, could withstand the terrible impetuosity of the West Saxon Foot, and when the sun set, after a stout hand-to-hand fight that had lasted all day, Ceawlin was victor; the Kingdom of Wessex was firmly established.'

The Ridgeway Path runs through the centre of the Castle and emerges at a break in the ramparts on the far side. It then descends to meet the 'Ridgeway proper' at a multiway junction. A disc barrow is on your right as you leave the castle; you will see this quite clearly as you head up towards the massive beech clumps on Hackpen Hill.

The Broad Hinton road is crossed 1½ miles from Barbury. On the right, but out of sight of the Ridgeway, is Hackpen Horse, cut into the hillside. You can approach it by walking along a path starting from the junction of the road with the Ridgeway. The Horse was cut in 1838 by the parish clerk of nearby Broad Hinton to commemorate the coronation of Queen Victoria. In a little more than one mile the

85

Ridgeway makes a sharp right-hand turn; then after a few yards turns left to resume its original direction.

You will shortly pass a large sarsen stone beside the track: a token of the Ridgeway's entry into the prehistoric metropolis centred round Avebury. From here you can see Avebury 2 miles south-west in the Kennett valley. If you are equipped with binoculars you will also see

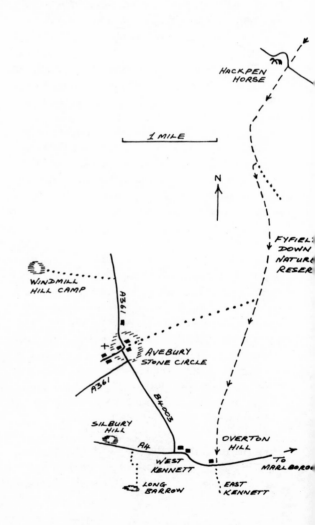

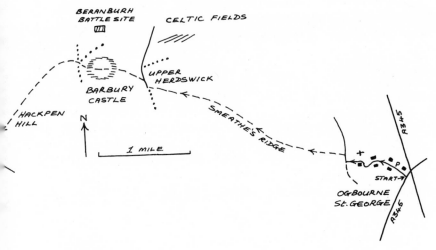

from this part of the Ridgeway an important archaeological site on
Windmill Hill, some 2½ miles eastward (see Historical Notes). For
a closer view Windmill Hill can be reached from Avebury Trusloe
or from the A361 road 1 mile north of Avebury.

Continuing along the Ridgeway you will pass an entrance to Fyfield
Down National Nature Reserve (see Historical Notes). Overton Hill
– the end of the Ridgeway Path will then be little more than 2 miles
away. Numerous barrows, many of them tree-covered, accompany
the Path along this final stretch. The planting of trees on barrows
and high points on the Downs was a fashionable 19th-century pastime;
it served no practical purpose whatsoever and is understandably de-
plored by archaeologists. Now to an important 20th century settlement
on the A4: the Ridgeway Cafe!

Opposite the cafe, on the south side of the A4, is the site of a
Neolithic structure called The Sanctuary. All you will see are small
concrete blocks marking the positions of holes which once held stones
and wooden posts. The Sanctuary was linked to the Avebury stone
circle by Kennett Avenue – an avenue of stones that has now largely
disappeared.

Returning to Ogbourne: Bus 49 from Avebury, West Kennett and
East Kennett to Marlborough; about 2 journeys a day only (better
to phone for a taxi!). The nearest bus stop is ½ mile west from

87

Overton Hill – at West Kennett. Bus route 70 from Marlborough to Ogbourne is hourly, Mon-Sat only.

Historical Notes

Avebury: This village is partly enclosed by a great circle of sarsen stones brought from the downs. It is thought that the circle, together with two inner circles and a vast outer ditch, was constructed by immigrant Beaker peoples between the Late Stone Age and the Early Bronze Age (1800 BC or thereabouts), and used as an outdoor temple or ceremonial meeting place. Avebury is an attractive village in its own right and has a museum housing a collection of local archaeological finds.

Windmill Hill: The Hill has given its name to an ancient culture that was brought to this country from the continent by a race of Neolithic men around 3000 BC. The site is formally classified as a Neolithic causewayed camp: it has – or rather had – three concentric circular ditches crossed at intervals by causeways. Opinions differ as to its function, but it seems likely that it was used either as an enclosure for cattle or pigs or as a trading centre.

Fyfield Down: This is 'one of the largest and finest unreclaimed tracts of high chalk grassland left in England'. Being an area noted for its many sarsen stones, which in themselves are of considerable interest, it is with good reason that the Down was set aside as a Reserve by the Nature Conservancy in 1956. It is noted for wild plants and animals that can take advantage of the relatively undisturbed environment. For the historian there is a wealth of interest in the primitive field systems which cover much of the reserve. Permits are normally required for visitors wishing to visit the reserve, other than along public footpaths.

The Sanctuary: The purpose of the Sanctuary can only be guessed at, but the possibility that it had some kind of ritualistic function cannot be ruled out. It is very unfortunate that here, as elsewhere, personal gain and short-sightedness brought destruction to a valuable archaeological site: in the 19th-century a local farmer was named as having removed the stones in order to build a house in nearby Beck-hampton. Even more incredible is the record of a Marlborough doctor who scoured the land hereabouts (presumably the barrows, of which there are many) for human remains. He ground the bones into pow-der, and used this to produce what was, or so he claimed, a successful medicine!

Silbury Hill: This is a massive mound beside the A4, one mile west-ward from Overton Hill. With its 130ft summit and 5½ acre base it is the largest man-made mound in Europe – excluding slag heaps and the like, of course! The purpose of the hill is unknown; in spite of numerous excavations it has not revealed its secret. It was constructed in the late Neolithic period, about 2100 BC and took an estimated 5000 man-years to build. Almost opposite Silbury Hill a path leads southwards from the A4 to the West Kennett Long Barrow – an important chambered tomb dating back to about 2700 BC.

Appendix

Rail and Buses

Rail and bus links with towns and villages lying on or close to the Ridgeway Path. Rail and bus services are subject to change, so it is advisable to check on routes and times before setting out.

Ivinghoe Beacon: Bus 61 from Tring (town); 2-hourly, Mon-Sat and Sun p.m.

Tring Station: On the Euston-Milton Keynes line; hourly service every day. The station is on the Ridgeway Path, 1½ miles from the town.

Tring (town): Green Line coach 768 from London (Victoria) runs hourly, Mon-Sat only.

Wendover: On the Marylebone to Aylesbury line; hourly Mon-Sat. On Sunday use the Metropolitan line from Baker Street, and change at Amersham for hourly train to Wendover.

Princes Risborough: On the Marylebone to Banbury line; hourly Mon-Sat., 2-hourly Sunday.

Chinnor: Bus 331/332 from High Wycombe. 2-hourly, Mon-Sat only. High Wycombe station is on the same line as Princes Risborough.

Watlington: Bus 201 from Oxford; 2-hourly, Mon-Sat only. (Oxford Bus Company).

Nuffield and Wallingford: Citylink coach 390/490 from London (Victoria); 2-hourly every day.

Goring and Streatley: On the Paddington-Oxford line; hourly Mon-Sat., 2-hourly Sunday (change at Reading).

Wantage: Bus 302 from Didcot and Oxford; hourly, Mon-Sat only. Didcot and Oxford stations are on the same line as Goring and Streatley.

Wanborough and Ashbury: Bus 47 from Swindon; 2-hourly, Mon-Sat only.

Ogbourne St George and Marlborough: Bus 70 from Swindon; hourly, Mon-Sat only.

Swindon: is on the Paddington-Bristol/South Wales line; frequent service.

Bus Company Addresses

Routes 28 & 61/X61: Red Rover Buses, Bicester Road, Aylesbury, Bucks., HP19 3AL. Tel: Aylesbury (0296) 28001.

Routes 55/56/57: Aylesbury Bus, Buckingham Street, Aylesbury, Bucks., HP20 2LH. Tel: Aylesbury (0296) 84919.

Routes 501 & 768: London Country Bus Ltd., St Albans Road, Garston, Herts., WD2 6NN. Tel: Watford (0293) 673121.

Routes 323/324 and 331/332: The Bucks Berks Bus Company Ltd., The Bus Station, High Wycombe, Bucks., HP11 2HU. Tel: High Wycombe (0494) 20941.

Routes 5, 390/490 & 201: Oxford Bus Company, 395 Cowley Road, Oxford, OX4 2DJ. Tel: Oxford (0865) 774611.

Route 302: South Midland Ltd., 56a High Street, Witney, Oxon., OX8 6HJ. Tel: Witney (0993) 76679.

Routes 47 & 49: Thamesdown Transport, Corporation Street, Swindon, Wilts. Tel: Swindon (0793) 23700.

Route 70: Swindon and District Buses, The Bus Station, Swindon, Wilts., SN1 1EA. Tel: Swindon (0793) 22243.

Taxi Services

Tring: M & H, tel: (99182) 5795. Tring & District, tel: (99182) 2705.

Wendover: Philby's, tel: (0296) 622195. Chilton Travel (Butler's Cross), tel: (0296) 624838.

Princes Risborough: Witcher's, tel: (08444) 4239.

Watlington: N.J. Sarney, tel: (049161) 2243.

Wallingford: Jim's, tel: (0491) 37236. Hill's, tel: (0491) 37022 and 37497.

Didcot: Harrold's, tel: (0235) 814321. Bob's, tel: (0235) 814679.

Wantage: Robert's, tel: (02357) 3503. Radio Taxis, tel: (02357) 68678.

Swindon: Calder, tel: (0793) 722222. Appollo, tel: (0793) 36696 and 619559.

Marlborough: Merlin, tel: (0672) 53890. Harley's, tel: (0672) 52786.

Accommodation

This is not an exhaustive list: for further addresses see the Ridgeway Information and Accommodation Guide mentioned in the Introduction.

Note that the name of the telephone exchange is given only when it differs from the name of the town or village.

Ivinghoe, Bucks. Youth Hostel, Old Brewery House. Tel: Cheddington (0296) 668251.

Tring, Herts. Mrs. Copley, The Hazels, Gamnel, New Mill. Tel: (0442) 890101.

Aston Clinton, Bucks. Mrs. Hall, The Haven, 7 Lower Icknield Way. Tel: Aylesbury (0296) 630751.

Halton, Bucks. Mrs. Broadley, Willow Cafe, Tring Road. Tel: Aylesbury (0296) 622112.

Wendover: Bucks. Mrs. Luck, 23 Chiltern Road. Tel: (0296) 623319. Mrs Biggs, The Hollies, Nash Lee Road. Tel: (0296) 623089.

Askett, Bucks. Mrs. Ramsay, The Bell House Barn, Crowbrook Road. Tel: Princes Risborough (08444) 6107.

Bradenham, Bucks. (2½ miles from Princes Risborough: 2-hourly train to Saunderton plus one mile walk, or infrequent bus). Youth Hostel, The Village Hall. Tel: Naphill (024024) 2929.

Bledlow, Bucks. Mrs Jeffery, The Gables, Skittle Green. Tel: Princes Risborough (08444) 4392.

Aston Rowant. Mrs. Dapling, Beacon Cottage, Aston Hill (A40 – on the Ridgeway Path). Tel: Kingston Blount (08444) 51219.

Watlington, Oxon. Mrs. Roberts, Cross Cottage, 48 High Street. Tel: (049161) 2218.

Nuffield, Oxon. Hayden Farm. Tel: Goring-on-Thames (0491) 64169.

Benson, Oxon. Mrs. Belcher, Hale Farm. Tel: Wallingford (0491) 36818.

Wallingford, Oxon. Mrs. MacKenzie, 25b St John's Road. Tel: (0491) 37402.

Goring, Oxon. Mrs. Wiltshire, Leyland, 3 Wallingford Road. Tel: (0491) 872119.

Streatley, Berks. Youth Hostel, Hill House. Tel: Goring (0491) 872278.

East Hendred, Oxon. Mrs. Newman, Ridgeway Lodge, Skeats Bush. Tel: Didcot (0235) 833360.

Wantage, Oxon. Court Hill Youth Hostel (on the downs 2 miles from Wantage). Tel: (02357) 60253.

Mrs. Krievs, 55 NewburyStreet. Tel: (02357) 67595.

Mrs. Kelleher, Maindy Lodge Guest House, 14 Charlton Road. Tel: (02357) 2813.

Uffington, Oxon. Mrs. Oberman, Norton House, Broad Street. Tel: (036782) 230.

Mrs. Wadsworth, The Craven, Fernham Road. Tel: (036782) 449.

Mrs. Matthews, Packers Forge, High Street. Tel: (036782) 244.

Wanborough Plain, Wilts. The Shepherds Rest, Foxhill Crossroads. Tel: Swindon (0793) 970266.

Ogbourne St George. Mrs. Edwins, Foxlynch. Tel: (067284) 307.

West Kennett, Wilts. The Ridgeway Cafe, Overton Hill. Tel: Lockeridge (067286) 234.

Winterbourne Monkton. Mrs. Randerson, Windmill House. Tel: Avebury (06723) 446.

Marlborough: Mrs. Harrison, 63 George Lane. Tel: (0672) 52771.

Youth Hostels. Details of YHA membership may be obtained from Trevelyan House, 8 St Stephen's Hill, St Albans, Herts., AL1 2DY. If you wish to 'give the YHA a try' before joining, you can do so by obtaining a Guest Pass on arrival at a hostel. Membership is open to anyone from age 5 upwards; and there's no *upper* age limit! Please refer to the YHA Guide for details of opening times – which vary from hostel to hostel. And whatever else you do, do visit Court Hill Hostel!

Camp Sites

Silver Birch Cafe, Pitstone. Tel: Cheddington (0296) 668348.

White Mark Farm, 82 Hill Road, Watlington. Tel: (049161) 2295.

Riverside Caravan and Camping Site, Crowmarsh. Tel: Wallingford (0491) 35351.

Britchcombe Farm, Woolstone (on the B4507 below Whitehorse Hill). Limited space only. Tel: Uffington (036782) 667.

Shepherds Rest, Fox Hill Crossroads, Wanborough. Tel: Swindon (0793) 790266.

Eating Out

Ivinghoe: The King's Head Restaurant.

Aldbury: Teas at one of the old cottages.

Tring: Foxy's Corner House, Frogmore Street. Indian and Italian restaurants in High Street. Two take-aways in Akeman Street. Teas at The Royal Hotel, Tring Station.

Wendover: The Landon, South Street. Anne Boleyn, Pound Street. The Coffee House, High Street.

Butler's Cross: Cream teas at the post office!

Princes Risborough: Fish Restaurant, Market Square. Mr. M's, Duke Street. Indian restaurant, High Street.

Watlington: The Well Hosue, High Street. Prince of India, Couching Street.

Wallingford: The Lamb Coffee Shop, High Street. Harriet's and The Baker's Oven, St Mary's Street.

North Stoke: Teas at the church on summer Sunday afternoons!

Goring: Riverside Tea Room. The Coffee Pot in The Arcade.

Wantage: Glensam Cafe and Epicure Restaurant, Grove Street. Chatterbox and Pizza Capri, Newbury Street,

Woolstone: Teas at Britchcombe Farm at weekends (on the B4507 below Whitehorse Hill).

Ogbourne St George: St George's Cafe and Robin Hood Restaurant.

Overton Hill: Ridgeway Cafe.

In addition to the above, there are good public houses, many of which serve meals, to revive the walker.